Blueswomen:
Profiles of 37 Early Performers,
with an Anthology of Lyrics,
1920–1945

To my blues buddies,
Martin Bourgeois and Jeff Childress,
and Mom and Dad

Blueswomen

*Profiles of 37 Early Performers,
with an Anthology of Lyrics,
1920–1945*

Anna Stong Bourgeois

McFarland & Company, Inc., Publishers
Jefferson, North Carolina, and London

Acknowledgments

The author thanks Thomas Barden for all of his insightful input on this project. Without his generous gifts of time and patience, this book would not have been possible. I would also like to acknowledge Ohio's Bowling Green State University Music Library especially Bill Shurk, for the loan of the songs that appear in this anthology. This project could not have even been started if not for their gift of music, as women's blues songs such as the ones addressed here are extremely rare. I thank Martin Bourgeois, Lisa Finley and Juli Forsthoefel for all of their help with the tedious research at the Library of Congress. Their aid in obtaining valuable information, along with their wonderful support and interest, made this project feasible as well as enjoyable. Finally, I would like to thank Ann Bourgeois, Lisa Kotnik and many other friends who contributed in transcribing some of the more difficult lyrics.

British Library Cataloguing-in-Publication data are available

Library of Congress Cataloguing-in-Publication Data

Bourgeois, Anna Stong.
    Blueswomen : profiles of 37 early performers, with an anthology of lyrics, 1920–1945 / by Anna Stong Bourgeois.
       p.   cm.
    Includes bibliographical references and index.
    ISBN 0-89950-963-0 (lib. bdg. : 50# alk. paper) ∞
    1. Blues (Music) — Texts.   2. Blues musicians — United States —
Biography.   3. Women singers — United States — Biography.   I. Title.
ML54.6.B79B6   1966 <Case>
782.42'1643'0922 — dc20
[B]   96-1158
                                       CIP
                                     MN

Manufactured in the United States of America

McFarland & Company, Inc., Publishers
Box 611, Jefferson, North Carolina 28640

Table of Contents

v

Preface

Women blues singers have never been as celebrated as their male counterparts, for reasons that are not entirely clear. Their songs are less widely known, their names are less famous, and their lives have seldom been written about. In fact, until now there has never been an anthology devoted solely to women's blues lyrics, despite the existence of at least two such books of men's blues lyrics (both compiled by Jeff Todd Titon).

The women of the blues are numerous and talented, and they deserve better than second-class status. They have lived fascinating lives and produced compelling music that reveals an often ignored side of the cultural experience out of which the blues grew. In this book I have attempted to collect a fair representation of their words and tell something of their lives. Thirty-seven of the most important women blues singers of the period from 1920 to 1945 — the first and greatest flowering of the blues — are profiled herein with concise biographies and a selection of complete song lyrics.

I am deeply indebted to the Bowling Green State University Music Library in Bowling Green, Ohio, where this project began. Their collection of music holdings is so complete that I was able to find numerous songs performed by women blues singers, including many obscure singers who are not widely known. Once I had access to all of their women's blues between 1920 and 1945, I began transcribing the lyrics with the help of friends on the more difficult passages. Since I was listening to original recordings, many of which were of poor quality, some words were not decipherable. In such instances, I placed parentheses around what I thought to be the lyrics.

While I collected virtually all of the women's blues held by the Bowling Green State University Music Library, many of the songs were still under copyright and could not appear in this anthology. The songs included either were never copyrighted or have lapsed into the public domain because their copyrights were not renewed. In order to find information about copyrights, each song was researched at the Library of Congress in Washington, D.C. Lists of song lyrics that were not renewed or were never copyrighted may be found in the appendices. Since it was not possible to include a complete collection of lyrics for each woman blues singer mentioned in this anthology, those who are interested in obtaining further information about the songs performed by these singers should refer to Robert M.W. Dixon and John Godrich's *Blues and Gospel Records: 1902–1943* (Essex: Storyville Publications, 1982), as this source contains a complete discography of blues performed by both men and women.

The Library of Congress was a good resource for biographical information, especially in the case of the more obscure singers. But the lack of information on some female composers and singers accentuates the fact that in the blues genre, women have not always been seriously considered.

Once again women's blues are becoming very popular. Boxed sets of complete collections of Bessie Smith and collections of women's blues are available at many record stores. With the increasing popularity of women's blues comes an interest in studying the lyrics to the songs and learning about the lives of the women who sang the blues. Both are fertile subjects for further study.

Introduction

When a woman gets the blues, she wrings her hands and cries
I said, When a woman gets the blues, she wrings her hands and cries,
But when a man gets the blues, he grabs a train and rides.
When a woman gets the blues, she goes to her room and hides.
When a woman gets the blues, she goes to her room and hides.
But when a man gets the blues, he catch a freight train and rides
   [Smith, "Freight Train Blues"].

My man done left me, quit me for another woman, rode the train out of town, left a note said he won't be back, I don't know where to find 'im but I will hop the train and find 'im and when I do I'll shoot 'im on the spot. For now, ain't got nothin' to ease my blues but moonshine whiskey, dope, cocaine, cigarettes and singing. Gotta sell myself for money, house rent's due, walk the street to earn a home but not in time 'cause the landlord's done evicted me already. Try to find a job but the white man only wants the light skins, can't sleep, can't dream. Got sickness, death, pain all around me don't know what to do, go to the gypsy get me a mojo hand and black cat bone ease my misery. Trouble follow me, trouble carry me to my grave.

Women blues singers proclaim their pain through songs. Blues lyrics like the ones above are found throughout women's blues songs, and the women's helplessness is partially overcome by these verbal expressions of their torment and troubles. So many times women have been forced to remain silent, and the blues have offered a needed and well deserved release for the emotional trauma that is a part of everyday life. For women, the blues have not only been an escape, but a chance to speak up, to protest the injustice and heartache in their lives. The voices of the women express a desire for freedom and equality in a time when women were almost universally told to shut up and mind their own business.

1

But these voices will not always be silenced. While most research in the area of the blues deals with men, more and more people are becoming interested in women's blues, and as a result, their voices and the details of their life stories will endure.

An old blues line says, "You can't sing the blues until you've paid your dues." This statement defines the blues singer's story. Just as male blues singers sing of the blues that derive from homesickness (the men were often ramblers), trouble with the law, and trouble with their women, female blues singers portray these and other aspects of their misery in their emotional blues songs. The poetry of women's blues reflects hardships ranging from sickness and disease to dependence on their mistreating men and suggests that the cultural conditions for the men and women were somewhat different. These differences are captured by the themes, musical style and subject matter of women's blues songs.

In order to glean the essence of the blues sung by women, it is necessary to envision oneself in a similar situation. Picture this: born into a family of eight children in a desolate log cabin with dirt floors, you are one of five girls. Money, food and medical supplies are very hard to come by. In the South, segregation and discrimination abound, and the only professions available for you, a girl of thirteen, are prostitute, housewife, or singer. Your family needs money, so at age thirteen you choose the more glamorous of the careers and set out to sing on the vaudeville circuit. Your life is tough; a young black woman has little control over political or social affairs. All a black girl may do to alleviate the anxieties and pressures of an otherwise invisible personality is sing the blues. The blues for a young African American woman are hatred, animosity and despair internalized and transformed into songs which live on today.

The poetry of the woman blues singer during this time period centers on sexism and racism. The black woman, who is perceived lower on the social hierarchy than even the black man, encounters prejudice in many forms. It is only natural that such an oppressed people would reveal the cause of their suffering in their folklore, which is largely accounted for in the blues verse. Ralph Ellison, who recognizes that there is "no dichotomy between art and protest" (1972, 169), explains the relationship between the lives of women performers and their blues music:

> The clue to this (what in African American culture is worth preserving or abandoning) can be found in folklore, which offers the first drawings of any group's character. It preserves mainly those situations which have been repeated again and again in the history of any given group.

It describes those rights, manners, customs and so forth, which ensure the good life, or destroy it; and it describes those boundaries of feeling, thought and action which that particular group has found to be the limitation of the human condition [1972, 171].

It is not surprising that women blues performers, who comprise a folk group in and of themselves, would sing about such pertinent lifestyle issues in their lamenting blues songs.

Women's blues lyrics can be divided into different categories based on theme. A common theme proclaimed is the nature of relationships between men and women. Within this category are subjects such as murdering one's spouse, lonesomeness emerging from a lover's desire to ramble, and physical and mental abuse occurring in unsatisfactory love affairs. Oppression stemming from sexism and racism prompts women blues singers to produce songs of superstition, wherein they discuss issues of luck and the necessity of gypsies or fortune tellers. The superstitious songs function to provide meaning in an otherwise helpless environment. Other categories of blues themes include replies to unconcealed racism, unjust work environments, and the consumption of drugs and alcohol as a relief for social problems. These common themes are relative to the society and culture in which the blues women lived.

Relationships

Well, there ain't no love, there ain't no gettin' along.
Well, there ain't no love, there ain't no gettin' along.
I found he treats me so mean sometimes I don't know right from
  wrong [Smith, "Every Woman's Blues"].

I was just your slave, I loved and worshipped you [Hunter, "I Won't
Let You Down"].

Some of the figures of oppression clamping down on the lives of these women are physically and mentally domineering men. In blues songs, many women complain about the singlemindedness of their cheating, mistreating, gambling spouses. They are disgusted with their husbands or paramours, so they sing about the challenges of forced relationships and are not afraid to criticize their spouses in cunning ways. Women rebel by threatening their lovers with ultimatums:

> Hey, what's that I heard you say?
> Hey, what's that I heard you say?
> You are going away and leave me today.
>
> If you go away and leave me today,
> If you go away and leave me today,
> Said you can't come back so you had better stay
> [Martin, "Useless Blues"].

or proverbial lessons:

> Here's a little lesson I want you to learn.
> Here's a little lesson I want you to learn.
> That if you play with fire you are sure to get burned
> [Martin, "Useless Blues"].

Other women blues singers dare to end their misery by killing their spouse, as Ma Rainey suggests in her song "Tough Luck Blues":

> My friend committed suicide, I've got to wait and see.
> My friend committed suicide, I've got to wait and see.
> They want to lock me up for him

Here, Ma Rainey admits that she may be charged with murder in the killing of her lover, and her mere suggestion of this charge insinuates her guilty conscience for having committed the crime.

Not all women consider homicide when dealing with their impossible spouses. Hociel Thomas uncovers a creative act of violence which stops short of murder:

> Catch you in deep waters, tear your eyeballs out ["Deep Water Blues"].

But when killing does become an option for escape, women most often choose poison or small guns for murder weapons. Spivey's "Blood Hound Blues" portrays a poisonous homicide:

> Well, I poisoned my man, I put it in his drinking cup,
> Well, I poisoned my man, I put it in his drinking cup,
> Well, it's easy to go to jail, but Lawd they sent me up.

And in "Murder in the First Degree" Spivey recalls a gun as the method of destruction:

> My man got runnin' around with a woman he know I can't stand.
> My man got runnin' around with a woman he know I can't stand.
> That's why I got my gun and got rid of one triflin' man.

In the blues lyric, women reserve the act of murder almost exclusively for the mistreating lover.

Breakups in relationships cast the majority of blame on the male spouse. Women insist most often that men leave them abandoned during their rambling expeditions, and Clara Smith begs for her companion to come home in her song "Tell Me When":

> Please tell me, tell me, won't you tell me when?
> The time that evening train pulls in.
> Tell me when, tell me when, Lawdy won't you tell me when?

Smith alleges that her man has left her, and lays the cause of her lonesomeness on her absent lover.

Some women accuse their lover of spending all their rent money on drugs, as does Lucille Bogan in "Pothound Blues":

> Now you take your money, you have your fun.
> You don't have nothin' when high rent come.
> And I'm through, cookin' your stew and beans.
> And you can eat more neck bones than any man I ever seen.

Bogan lays the blame for the problems in this relationship solely on her pothound boyfriend.

Another complaint is that the men constantly cheat on their innocent wives, and Victoria Spivey relays this in "Give It to Him":

> To my fullest satisfaction I have learned that men like action.
> But that doesn't mean that you should go and cheat on me.

Spivey admits an understanding for her stereotypically sexually active male lover, but expresses her disapproval at his attempt to carry out all of his sexual impulses.

Women such as Edith Wilson speak out against men who become lazy and neglect to perform the duties that they believe only a man can do:

> Once I used to brag about my handy man,
> But I ain't braggin' no more.
> Something strange has happened to my handy man,
> He's not the man he was before.
> I wish someone could explain to me about this dual personality.
> He don't perform his duty like he used to do.
> He never hauls the ashes 'less I tell him to.
> Before he hardly gets to work he's gettin' through.
> My handy man ain't handy no more
> ["My Handy Man Ain't Handy No More"].

Not only is Wilson constrained within marital boundaries, she also limits herself; the source of her oppression is both internal and external. Another woman who follows Wilson's role is Clara Smith, whose song "Ain't Got Nobody to Grind My Coffee" strongly emphasizes a need for a man in the house:

> Once I had a lovin' daddy, just as sweet as he could be.
> But my ever lovin' daddy, he's done gone from me.
> And since he's left me behind, guess what's on my mind.
> I ain't got nobody to grind my coffee in the morning.

Many times women blues performers felt themselves trapped in a no-win situation; they were unhappy with their mistreating spouses, but they believed themselves to be emotionally and physically dependent on them.

In terms of their physical relationships, women blues singers discuss their need or desire for intimacy. But women performers differentiate from male performers on this topic, as they must use euphemisms to cover promiscuous language. When talking about sex, women will do so covertly, as does Lucille Bogan in her song "New Way Blues,"

> It's a new way of lovin', and everybody can't catch on.
> It's a new way of lovin', and everybody can't catch on.
> But if you do it like I tell you, you sure, Lord, can't go wrong.

By using the terms "new way of lovin'," Bogan implies a new style of sexual intercourse in a way that is not considered offensive. Cleo Gibson uses the same style to talk about sex in "I've Got Movements in My Hips," as she says:

> I got Ford Engine movements in my hips,
> 10,000 miles guaranteed.
> I say, 10,000 miles guaranteed.

By referring to "movements in her hips," Gibson obviously alludes to the hip movements that occur during sexual encounters.

Other women use suggestive language throughout their songs, but at the end of the song, they qualify their language by attaching a different meaning to the sex that they have been indirectly speaking of. An example of this may be found in Alberta Hunter's "Take Your Big Hands Off It," in which Hunter appears to be talking about her virginity:

> I got a pretty something a lot of cats would like to get.
> But I won't let em' have it cause it hasn't been used yet.

So take your big hands off it ooh, but wouldn't you like to have it.
They're plenty of others just like you.
You swear you're gonna get it, Well you'll never live to tell it.
'Cause I'm savin' it for a man that's true.

Hunter uses the common cliché of saving one's virginity for the right
man, and by doing so, suggests that she is deliberating on whether or not
to have sex. However, the end of her song relays a different message:

I'm talkin' 'bout my big red rose.
It's too delicate for you.
I'm talkin' bout this big red rose.
Ain't that a shame?

Hunter tries to deny the sexual undertones that have so far prevailed by
saying that she has been talking about her rose. But the suggestive language throughout the song counteracts this end confession, leaving us
well aware of what she has so carefully implied.

Rosa Henderson uses this same method in "Get It Fixed" as the "it"
that she mentions is her lover's penis. While the women singers often
express discontent in their relationships with men, they will, in many
instances, admit that they crave the love that their partners give them.
Henderson exemplifies this:

Papa, papa better strut your stuff.
Daddy, Daddy, but don't be too rough.
Mama wants some love and kisses right away.
Want 'em when I want 'em honey, don't delay ["Get It Fixed"].

The women may suffer physical and verbal abuse, but they often remain
with their lovers for a small amount of comfort and companionship.

Drugs and Alcohol

Sippie Wallace explains her mental addiction to alcohol:

I'm gonna get drunk, papa just one more time.
Oh, daddy, just one more time.
'Cause when I'm drunk, nothin' don't worry my mind
["Dead Drunk Blues"],

as does Bessie Smith:

The man I love, he done left this town.
The man I love, he has a left this town.
And if it keeps snowin' I will be drunk all the time
["Gulf Coast Blues"].

Alcohol helps the women to forget about their unhappy life situations. Many women even strive to lose control under the effects of intoxication:

When I get drunk who's gonna take me home?
'Cause when I get drunk I don't know right from wrong.
I been in a trouble oh baby believe it's true.
That's why I got those gut struggle blues [Davis, "Gut Struggle"].

Davis is not ashamed to admit that she is willing to drink herself into a stupor in order to lessen her blues.

The record titles "Weed, a Rare Batch" and "Pot, Spoon, Pipe and Jug" signify the predominant tendency toward drug usage. In "If You're a Viper (Weed, a Rare Batch)," Lorraine Walton blatantly sings of the effects of marijuana:

When your throat gets dry, you know you're high.
Everything is dandy and you truck on down to the candy store.
Bust your cunk on peppermint candy.
Then you know your brown body's spent.
You don't care if you don't pay rent.
Sky's high but so am I, if you're a viper.

Walton depicts the common characteristics of marijuana usage from an unquenchable thirst to an increased appetite and laid back personality.

Ella Fitzgerald is blunt about her discussion of the need for drugs in "When I Get Low, I Get High," and she explains her addiction:

All this hard luck in this town has found me.
Nobody knows how trouble goes round and round me.
I said, when I get low oh oh oh oh oh oh I get high.

Hazel Myers admittedly dreams about a full marijuana pipe, suggesting her complete obsession with drugs:

But when I awoke, my heart almost broke.
Dreamed I had a pot pipe in my hand.
Had a full damn pot pipe in my hand.

Myers is devastated when she awoke to the realization that she was only dreaming about her found treasure. Drugs and alcohol provided an escape in the form of an altered state which was more comfortable in its haziness.

Illness and Disease

Every man I get if he don't get sick he will die [Minnie, "I'm a Bad Luck Woman].

Given the amount of reported drug usage, the lack of food and medicine, and inadequate living conditions among members of this folk group, it is not unusual that the women performers complained about illness. A common ailment discussed is tuberculosis. Victoria Spivey deals with the misery of this often fatal disease in "T.B.'s Got Me":

T.B.'s got me, and all my friends are throwin' me down.
But they treated me so nice when I had the paper to run around.

Oh, my poor lungs are hurtin' me so.
Mmmmm, my poor lungs are hurtin' me so.
I don't get no peace or comfort no matter where I go.

Spivey's quest for "peace" and "comfort" is always denied, as crowded living arrangements restrict the privacy that would help in renewing her health. Spivey again mentions lung disease in "Dopehead Blues," in which she also portrays her dependence on dope to help her forget her ailment:

Got double pneumonia and still I think I got the best health.

Conceivably, the excessive use of marijuana combined with cigarette smoking perpetuates the lung problems which prevail among these women. Whatever the cause for such illnesses, the women express a feeling of helplessness when dealing with disease which may partially explain their reliance on superstition.

Superstition

Gypsies, mojos, black cats, and lucky numbers provide common means for understanding the world. Many times the mojo is called on for help in love or for relieving illnesses. The mojo and other superstitious devices help to give the believer an illusion of control in what are otherwise perceived to be helpless situations. In "Fogyism," Ida Cox explains her ability to foresee death:

> Why do people believe in some old signs?
> Why do people believe in some old signs?
> To hear a hoodoo holler, someone is surely dyin'.

The sign of the "hoodoo holler" renders death more predictable and so more controlled.

Many times the women singers rely on luck rather than on their own ability to change their life situations. Ida Cox reveals many of the common luck superstitions throughout the remainder of "Fogyism":

> Some will break a mirror, cry about bad luck for seven years.
> Some will break a mirror, cry about bad luck for seven years.
> And if a black cat crosses them, they'll break right down in tears.
>
> To dream of muddy water, trouble's knockin' at your door.
> To dream of muddy water, trouble is knockin' at your door.
> Your man is sure to leave you and never return no more.

The belief in luck functions as a defense for people, as the responsibility or blame for undesirable occurrences may be diffused, and luck may help to explain why unfortunate situations arise. Other superstitious fortunes such as "When a gator hollers, some folks say it's gonna rain" supply the world with a sense of order.

The women blues singers are so affected by superstitions that they believe in the power of the snake tamer; a snake tamer possesses the ability to tame and hypnotize snakes as well as individuals. Clara Smith recognizes this immense power in her song "Daddy Don't Put That Thing on Me," when she pleads with her snake taming boyfriend to leave her alone:

> I know a big handsome papa, called the snake charming king.
> A man that loves to chauffeur that big black thing.
> He's just as right as any man can be.
> But he loves to put that thing on children like me.
> Guess what I'll say if I just see him start comin' my way.
> Oh, don't you dare to put that thing on me.

Smith recognizes the snake charmer's power but begs that she will be spared from his attempt to gain total reign over her mind. Even the title to this song uncovers the widespread acceptance of superstition, as many people believed that spells could be cast or "put" on them.

Memphis Minnie sums up the need for a belief in luck as a form of superstition in her song "I'm a Bad Luck Woman":

> Well the next man I got bought me a hat and a dress.
> And every time I look around the police had him on a doggone
>   arrest.
> I'm a bad luck woman, I'm a bad luck woman, I'm a bad luck woman
>   I can't see the reason why.

Living in a time when nothing seems to go their way, the women contrive a belief in luck to help themselves figure out why bad situations seem to follow them. If a woman gets sick, ends up alone because of a rambling spouse, or loses her job, it is all on account of bad luck. Almost every impossible or negative occurrence may be categorized as a bad luck happenstance.

Work

When discussing work, women performers talk about the unfavorable working environments that their husbands or lovers must deal with. This is perhaps most evident in the song "Log Camp Blues," performed by Ma Rainey, which subtly suggests that the pay for a man who works in a log camp is quite inadequate. When Rainey sings:

> Melons in my meat box, chicken runs around my yard.
> Melons in my meat box, chicken runs around my yard.
> Youngens in my coffin, I never knews the time was hard,

it is suggested that if her husband brought home more pay, she may have had enough food to keep her children alive; she may have had meat in her meat box rather than melons if her spouse were treated fairly.

The main profession that the blues women sing about is prostitution, and many performers discuss this trade either deliberately or inadvertently. Memphis Minnie sings of the trade without shame in "Hustlin' Woman Blues,"

> I sit on the corner all night long,
> Counting the stars one by one.
> Sit on the corner all night long,

Counting the stars one by one.
I didn't make no money, oh and then I can't go back home,

and in so doing, she shows the unfair and cruel treatment she receives from her pimp:

My man stops in the window with a .45 in his hand.
My man stops in the window with a .45 in his hand.
Every now and then he gets up and hollers at me, and tells me,
 "you better not miss that man."

Working conditions for both African American men and women were poor, but even more so for the women, as they had fewer choices to make in pursuing their careers.

Other women blues performers are more discreet in their discussion of prostitution. Irene Scruggs' "Must Get Mine in Front" reveals the life of a woman named Susie who supposedly runs a bakery. The key to understanding this song as one about prostitution resides in the types of doughnuts she sells, which are "jelly rolls." This is a common euphemism for vagina used by women. Scruggs reveals the tricks of prostitution:

She looked at him and said "Don't be no ham.
What kind of fool do you think I am? Some folks may trust you,
 some, I can't say. I must get mine in front. I'll trust you tomorrow
 if you pay me today. I must get mine in front."

When Scruggs explains that Susie "must get hers in front," she means that Susie will not trust someone to pay her tomorrow for a trick performed today.

The women performers are not happy about being prostitutes, but most often the money they make on the street is essential for survival. Women may become streetwalkers to support their lovers or their children, or to pull enough money together to pay the rent. In Georgia White's "Walkin' the Street" she gives her reason for prostitution:

I've got these street walkin' blues, I ain't got no time to lose.
I've got these street walkin' blues, I ain't got no time to lose.
I've got to make six dollars just to buy my man a pair of shoes.

Chippie Hill sings about resorting to prostitution to pay the rent:

Stood on the corner, till my feet are soakin' wet.
Stood on the corner, till my feet are soakin' wet.
Singin' the street walkin blues, to each and every one I met.

Baby, if you ain't got a dollar, give me just one lousy dime.
If you ain't got a dollar, give me just one lousy dime.
'Cause the landlord's singin', just because my rent's behind.

Prostitution was common, and even though the profession was undesirable, her body was all a poor woman had to sell.

Racism

Racism in women's blues lyrics is multi-dimensional. Intraracial prejudice is uncovered almost to the same degree as interracial prejudice. Some women protest unfair discrimination based on skin color, and Alberta Hunter's song, "You Can't Tell the Difference After Dark" comically expresses uneasiness at such discrimination:

They say that gentlemen prefer blonde ladies.
Tell me, am I out of style, just because I'm slightly shady?
Just wait until I've won ya, and my love looks down upon ya.
You can't tell the difference after dark.

Hunter criticizes people who are shallow and believe that physical appearance is of utmost importance.

But other women blues singers judge people on their skin color. In "How Long, Daddy, How Long," Ida Cox says:

It takes a brown skinned man to run a woman insane.

Cox subscribes to the commonly held stereotype that the lighter the skin a person has the more socially and physically desirable he or she is. Issie Ringgold makes a similar racist statement in "Be on Your Merry Way," when she says, "But you ain't gonna park in my brown skinned bed." The lighter or brown skinned African American was given an undeniable preference. Clara Smith mentions the priority given to the lighter skinned people in "Every Woman's Blues":

I haven't the heart to tell him to his face
that some other good brown has taken his place.

The word "brown" is here associated with the word "good," and this was an association that was accepted and agreed upon. In fact, many women shunned men of darker skin entirely, for fear that their offspring would be dark skinned. Lucille Bogan may be exemplifying this point in "New Way Blues," when she says:

> Did you ever get on brown skin and come up black?
> Did you ever get on brown skin and come up black?
> And did you ever get something that you really lack?

The phrase "come up black" signifies the fear of producing child with darker skin.

Racism that arises from the white culture is discussed with bitterness, and "Tennessee Workhouse Blues" performed by Jenny Pope fervently elaborates on this issue:

> He was charged with murder, but stealin' was his crime.
> He was charged with murder, but stealin' was his crime.
> He stole my daddy and had to serve his time.

Since the white man has total control over the African American in this environment, many people were allegedly convicted on trumped up charges. While Pope expresses her dismay at this terrible injustice:

> That workhouse, workhouse is way out on a lonesome road.
> That workhouse, workhouse is way out on a lonesome road.
> I hate to see my daddy carry that heavy load,

there is nothing that she may do to remedy the situation.

All of these themes give detailed reports of the culture from which these songs came. Because of this, women's blues song lyrics may be appreciated for more than their aesthetic value alone. They may be revered as historical documentations, no more distorted or biased than the accounts received in public high school history classes. These documentations are priceless, as they divulge information that may easily be lost in a patriarchal society. For example, if we were to rely on Alan Lomax's account of the female blues singers, we could only believe that "with few exceptions, only women in show business, only women of questionable reputation, women who flaunted their loose living, publicly performed the blues" (1993, 360). In his book *The Land Where the Blues Began*, Lomax makes several other unfounded and sexist remarks pertaining to the women blues singers such as "the blues have been mostly masculine territory" (1993, 358) and "down in the land where the blues began, the majority of real, sure enough, aspiring-to-be-professional blues singers — who, as they put it, 'followed the blues' — wore pants" (1993, 358). Lomax's account of the blues is biased toward males and is in fact partially untrue; in his story the challenges and talents of women blues singers are blatantly ignored. The only way that this sexism may be overcome is by digging up and acknowledging women's contributions to the blues.

The suffering, heartaches, and losses as well as the gladness and high times disclosed in women's blues lyrics are also valuable when studying and understanding African American literature. To understand the literature of a culture is to understand the lives that the authors lived. The blues theme is commonly encountered in literature of this genre, and blues lyrics furnish a direct source for those who are interested in African American literature.

It is evident that many African American writers are influenced by the blues. Langston Hughes demonstrates this influence in his poem entitled "Early Evening Quarrel," which reveals the experience of the black woman in the form of a blues poem. In this poem, Hughes' stanzas are like blues lyrics. In several areas in the poem, Hughes uses typical blues clichés. One stanza of this poem reads:

Lawd, these things we women
Have to stand!
I wonder is there nowhere a
Do-right man?

But Hughes is not the only African American writer who cites the blues. August Wilson's *Ma Rainey's Black Bottom: A Play in Two Acts* emerged as a direct response to Rainey's song with the same title.

Ralph Ellison is another author who has been heavily influenced by the blues. His book *Invisible Man* is considered a blues novel, and the theme of invisibility often emerges in blues songs. An example of invisibility in the blues is found in Robert Johnson's "Crossroad Blues." Johnson states, "Standin' at the crossroad, I tried to flag a ride. Didn't nobody know me, everybody pass me by." This passage from Johnson's song relates to a passage in *Invisible Man*, as Ellison describes his invisibility:

I am an invisible man. No, I am not a spook like those who haunted Edgar Allan Poe; nor am I one of your Hollywood-movie ectoplasms. I am a man of substance, of flesh and bone, fiber and liquids — and I might even be said to possess a mind. I am invisible, understand, simply because people refuse to see me [3].

The parallel between Ellison's conception of invisibility and Robert Johnson's notion of invisibility is irrefutable.

Many of the short stories and novels by Zora Neale Hurston contain blues themes. Since Hurston was writing during the time of the Harlem Renaissance, when blues songs were frequently heard in the bars and clubs in New York, it is probable that she too could have been influenced by the blues. Her story entitled "Sweat" certainly seems to suggest this possibility, as the theme of the story is much like the theme of the vaudeville songs. In this story, Delia is badly mistreated by her husband, Sykes, who repeatedly abuses her both verbally and physically. Thus, the story highlights the oppression of women during this time period in the same manner that the women's blues songs do. The song "Four Day Creep" by Ida Cox represents the infidelity of a mistreating spouse. Cox states, "Men are so doggone crooked, afraid he might make a four day creep." This statement characterizes the message found in a substantial number of blues songs which discuss the problems with male-female relationships.

Wallace Thurman's book entitled *The Blacker the Berry* addresses prejudice within the black race in much the same way Alberta Hunter addresses the issue in her song "You Can't Tell the Difference After Dark." Thurman satirizes the attitude of his character Maria, who joins the blue-vein circle for mulattos, while Hunter expresses her views in her upbeat blues song by saying, "I may be as brown as a berry but that's only secondary, and you can't tell the difference after dark."

Even Etheridge Knight, who wrote his poetry some years after the women blues singers in this anthology performed, appears to be influenced by the blues. His poem entitled "My Life, the Quality of Which," contains sentiments comparable to the feelings found in blues lyrics. Part of the poem is as follows:

> My life, the quality of which...
> IS
> and can be felt
> in the one word: DESPERATION
> But you have to *feel* for it [21].

The feeling of desperation is so often captured in blues songs that it is not possible to name all the lyrics here. However, if one examines the life situations of the female blues singers, the *feeling* of desperation is accounted for. Since most women blues performers had rough lives and lived through rocky relationships, it is easy to see how blues women could have "felt" the word desperation.

Women's blues lyrics depict life within this folk group in an honest, if sometimes exaggerated form. Each blues song contains a kernel of truth turned into story.

As long as there is oppression and injustice in the world, the blues song will always exist. Bemoaning misrepresentation, unfair working conditions, sexism, and racism, the blues will operate as a release for misery. And the blues will continue to make people happy. Whether it be through identification with another's problem or by expressing one's pain in a humorous or exaggerated fashion, the blues will be a creative outlet for those who search for relief.

I became enlightened to this theory when working in a bar in Toledo, Ohio. It is summertime, my uniform already sticks to me, and my five to twelve shift has just begun. I am a waitress; Saturday nights are especially long when the kitchen in the stuffy restaurant is fifteen degrees hotter than the extreme temperatures outside. The owner of the restaurant reeks of chauvinism. He is so macho with his black Saab (after all, he has an image to uphold) and car phone. Tonight he wears his silk shirt, and cigar ashes drop on him as he calls me to report to his table. When I am in the middle of taking an order he bellows, "Anna, come see me at the bar immediately!" As I walk over with intense dread, the shimmering tube of lipstick is then but a glimmer in his eye. "Put this on. Tell the other girls. I want you to wear this pink color."

Meanwhile, some customers at a table in station B want to know where their food is. The kitchen has lost their order, the bar is out of stock on their favorite beer. Other waitresses are becoming dismayed with the kitchen staff, who are working unnervingly slow in the sauna of a workroom. It is only seven o'clock and already all my co-workers are completely exasperated. Suddenly, an impulse has come over me. Blues songs are surging through my mind, and the song begins:

I got so many tables, I don't know what to do,
I got so many tables, I don't know what to do,
My boss is drinking ice cold beers that's why I got the blues.

I must wear this ugly lipstick, wear it all night long,
I must wear this ugly lipstick, wear it all night long,
As soon as twelve o'clock comes I'll be long, long gone.

Immediately, other waitresses chime in:

I got the waitressing blues, the waitressing blues,
I got the waitressing blues, the waitressing blues,
Change jigglin' in my pocket and ketchup on my shoes.

I got my tray in one hand, I got my pen in the other,
I got my tray in one hand, I got my pen in the other,
and I'm screamin' to a table, hold on a minute, brother!

The kitchen staff sing:

Gas oven is glowing, grease is on fire.
Gas oven is glowing, grease is on fire.
From this trashy bar we will never retire

Boss wants a steak done medium rare.
Boss wants a steak done medium rare.
Sure hope he don't find a long black hair.

It was not long before we were all laughing.

The Performers

——— Lucille Bogan ———

Lucille Bogan or Bessie Jackson was born April 1, 1897, in Monroe County, Mississippi and died August 10, 1948, in Los Angeles, California (Harris). Her last name was Anderson until she married Nazareth Bogan; during this marriage she bore two children (Harris).

Unlike her many peers, Bogan did not begin her career in the vaudeville circuit. She is referred to as showing a "predilection for crude stories about prostitution" (Herzhaft), and she differs from other female blues singers in that she does not attempt to cover up or euphemize songs that pertain to sex. A prime example of Bogan's crassness is the song "Shave 'Em Dry," which is in fact so crass that it was not released for public radio. From the beginning of this song which states, "I got nipples on my titties big as the end of my thumb, I got somethin' 'tween my legs would make a dead man come," it is evident that Bogan is completely uninhibited when reporting sexual activity. While Bogan recorded for OKEH, Paramount and Brunswick labels (Harris), "Shave 'Em Dry" was not released for public radio broadcastings because of its obvious obscenities.

Perhaps the difference between Bogan and her counterparts results from her lack of training on the vaudeville circuit; the women blues singers who were trained on vaudeville were expected to sing in a respectable manner.

Bogan died of coronary sclerosis in her own home, and she is buried at the Lincoln Memorial Park Cemetery, in Los Angeles, California (Harris).

"Tired As I Can Be"

I wait all the winter and I wait all fall.
I gotta wait until spring to get my ashes hauled.
And now I'm tired, tired as I can be.
And I'm goin' back home where these blues don't bother me.

I'm a free hearted woman, I let you spin my door.
And you never did win, you kept on askin' for more.
And now I'm tired, I ain't gonna do it no more.
And when I leave you this time you won't know where I go.

My house rent's due, they done put me outdoors.
And here you ridin' round here in a V8 Ford.
I done got tired of your low down dirty ways.
And your sister say you been dirty, dirty all your days.

I never will forget when the time was good.
I caught you standin' out yonder in the tiny woods.
And now I'm tired, tired as I can be.
And I'm goin' back south to my used to be.

"Shave 'Em Dry"

I got nipples on my titties, big as the end of my thumb.
I got somethin' 'tween my legs would make a dead man come.
Oh, who's that? Baby, won't you shave 'em dry?
Want you to grind me baby, grind me until I cry.

Say, I fucked all night and all the night before baby.
And I feel just like I want to fuck some more.
Oh, great God, daddy, honey, shave me till I'm dry.
And when you hear me holler, baby, want you to shave 'em dry.

I got nipples on my titties, big as the end of my thumb.
Daddy, you say that's the kind you want, and you can make 'em come.
Oh, daddy shave me dry.
And I'll give you somethin' baby, well, it'll make you cry.

I'm gonna turn back my mattress and let you oil my springs.
I want you to grind me, daddy, till the bells do ring.

Oh, daddy, want you to shave me dry.
Oh, great god daddy, if you can't shave 'em baby, won't you try.

Now, if fuckin' was a thing that would take me to hell,
I'd be fuckin' into you until the clock strikes twelve.
Oh, daddy, daddy shave 'em dry.
I would fuck you, baby, honey, I'd make you cry.

Now your nuts hang down like a damn bell clapper.
And your dick stands up like a stick.
Your goddamn asshole fell open like a church door,
and the crab walks in next to you.
Ow, shit! Woo, baby, won't you shave 'em dry.

A big sow gets fat from eatin' corn and a pig gets fat from suckin'.
When you see this poor fat black I am, great God, I got fat from
     fuckin'.
Woo, shave 'em dry.

My back is made of whale bone.
And my cock is made of brass.
And my fuckin' is made for workin' men's two dollars.
Great God, go round and kiss my ass.
Oh, woo, daddy, shave 'em dry.

"Stew Meat Blues"

A man say I have something, look like new.
He want me to credit him for some of my stew.
Say he's goin up the river, tryin' to sell his sacks.
He will pay me for the stuff when the boat gets back.
Now you can go on up the river, man, and sell your sacks.
You can pay me for my stew, when the boat gets back.

I got good stew and it's got to be sold.
Price ain't high I want to get you told.
Go on up the river, man, and sell your sacks.
there'll be stew meat here, baby when the boat gets back.

Now look here man, what you want me to do?
Give you my stew meat and credit you too.

You go on up the river, oh, and sell your sacks.
'Cause I'll have that stew meat here, when that boat gets back.

I credit one man, it was to my sorrow.
His cash today, credit tomorrow.
So, hurry up the river, baby, and try to sell your sacks.
There's gonna be meat here, when that boat gets back.

Now it's ashes to ashes, dust to dust.
You try my stuff one time you can't get enough.
So go on up the river, man and sell your stuff.
'Cause the stuff will be here, baby, when the boat gets back.

"Pay Roll Blues"

Pay day on the seventh, pay day on the yellow door.
Pay day on the seventh, pay day on the yellow door.
I want to meet that pay roll, and try to make a water hole.

Mens out on the seventh, they make dollars by the stack.
Mens out on the seventh, they make dollars by the stack.
And I'll have money in my sock, when that payroll train gets back.

I'm leavin' here broke, and I ain't got no money at all.
I'm goin' to leave here broke, and I ain't got no money at all.
But I will bet my life, I will make a water hole.

I will be startin' rollin', rollin' from town to town.
I will be startin' rollin', rollin' from town to town.
And I will have plenty money, when that four day roll is done.

You hear me beepin', money's what I've got to have.
You hear me beepin', money's what I've got to have.
I've got to get me fifty dollars if I have to make a midnight grave.

"New Way Blues"

Did you ever get on brown skin and come up black?
Did you ever get on brown skin and come up black?
And did you ever get something that you really lack?

Everybody is talkin', say I sure do know what to do.
Everybody is talkin', say I sure do know what to do.
And if you pay me my price, I'll learn that thing to you.

It's a new way of lovin', and everybody can't catch on.
It's a new way of lovin', and everybody can't catch on.
But if you do it like I tell you, you sure, Lord, can't go wrong.

Now, I want to bet my money, I've got a new way of gettin' down.
I want to bet my money, I've got a new way of gettin' down.
That I can get on black, but I'd sure love to come up brown.

Now there's a new way of lovin', this world is waitin' for.
There's a new way of lovin', this world is waitin' for.
And there's something about my lovin' that I ain't ever told.

"Pothound Blues"

Bring me a job or money from anywhere.
You must bring me a job or money from anywhere.
'Cause I can get your kinda lovin' in the streets just anywhere.

You come home every day lookin' for your stew and beans.
You come home every day lookin' for your stew and beans.
And you have got more nerve than any pothound I've ever seen.

Now you take your money, you have your fun.
You don't have nothin' when high rent come.
And I'm through, cookin' your stew and beans.
And you can eat more neck bones than any man I ever seen.

Now if you want me, baby, you got to make your first show down.
Now if you want me, baby, make your first show down.
And you got to put your money down where I got mine.

Now you layin' up in my bed, between my two white sheets.
I can't see or smell nothin' but your doggone feet.
And I'm through, tryin' to make a man of you.
And if you can't bring a job, don't you look for your daily stew.

I worked hard from Monday until late Saturday night.
And you're a dirty mistreater, you ain't treatin' me right.

And I'm through cookin' your stew and beans.
And you're a dirty pothound, dirtier than any man I seen.

"Groceries on the Shelf"

My name is Piggly Wiggly and I swear you can help yourself.
My name is Piggly Wiggly and I swear you can help yourself.
And you got to have your green back and it don't take nothin' else.

If Piggly Wiggly still here, Piggly Wiggly's everywhere.
Piggly Wiggly still here, Piggly Wiggly's everywhere.
If you don't find one here, you will find one over there.

You can go to your five, you can go to your ten cent store.
You can go to your five, you can go to your ten cent store.
But if you come to my Piggly Wiggly, you won't go back there no
    more.

No my friends all hate me 'cause I got a Piggly Wiggly store.
No my friends all hate me, got a Piggly Wiggly store.
I got roses on my shelf and they're layin' all over my floor.

Now my mama told me, papa told me too.
Said my mama told me, papa he told me too.
That the Piggly Wiggly store is goin' to be the ruin of you.

"Black Angel Blues"

I got a sweet black angel, I like the way he spread his wings.
I got a sweet black angel, I like the way he spread his wings.
And I'm crazy about him, he spreads so much joy in everything.

If I ask him for a dime, he give me a ten dollar bill.
If I ask him for a dime, he give me a ten dollar bill.
Yes, he does everything to keep my wants filled.

If my black angel would leave me, I believe that I would die.
If my black angel would leave me, I believe that I would die.
And if I see him lookin' at another woman, I just scream and cry.

I love my black angel and I want him by myself.
I love my black angel and I want him by myself.
Don't want him spreadin' his wings over nobody else.

Women don't bother my black angel, don't bother him in any way.
Women don't bother my black angel, don't bother him in any way.
I'll spend ninety-nine year in jail most any day.

I'm worried 'bout my black angel, I like the way he spread his wings.
I'm worried 'bout my black angel, I like the way he spread his wings.
He's got a new way of gettin' (spooked) and he sure can shake that
    thing.

"Coffee Grindin' Blues"

I drink so much coffee till I grind it in my sleep.
I drink so much coffee, I grind it in my sleep.
And when it get like that you know it can't be beat.

It's so doggone good and it make me bite my thumb.
It's so doggone good and it make me bite my thumb.
Gonna keep it for my daddy, ain't gonna give nobody none.

I ain't ever loved a this a way before.
I ain't ever loved a this a way before.
And I hope the Lord I won't love it anymore.

I've gotten so now that I can't control my mind.
I've gotten so now that I can't control my mind.
I go to bed blue and I get up cryin'.

It's so doggone good, it made me talk outa my head
It's so doggone good, it made me talk outa my head.
And it's better to me than any I've ever had.

Now I grind my coffee for two or three dollars a pound.
Now I grind my coffee for two or three dollars a pound.
And there ain't no more cheap like mine in town.

It's so doggone good until it made me talk outa my mind.
It's so doggone good, it made me talk outa my head.
And it's better to me than any I've ever had.

——Liza Brown——

Little is known about Liza (Eliza) Brown and Ann Johnson, the women who wrote the lyrics to "Get On Out of Here," appearing on the next page. Liza Brown's alias, Ozzie McPhearson, claims the original credits to "Get On Out of Here" according to Columbia files, but these names were crossed out (Dixon & Godrich). The song is a humorous dialogue centering around an argument between Brown and Johnson which takes place at a bar.

The argument exemplifies the competition between two women for a place in society. For example, one woman says to the other woman, "Every time I get a dance you come on up here and try to turn it out." At this point, the two women are in argument over a man; each wants to get the best man in the bar. Yet they are also in competition for jobs. When one woman says to the other, "Now don't be here when my pimp arrives, what I'll put on you gal you will be surprised," we see that the two women are also competing for tricks.

Most of the song is spoken except for the chorus, "Now take it on out of here, take it on out of here," and because of this, we may be receiving an actual depiction of what it was like for two women having a discussion in a bar setting. Women were constantly having to prove themselves and, rather than looking to other women for support, they often pitted against each other to raise their own stature.

"Get On Out of Here"
(All lines are spoken except those noted)

Hum, what you want to bring her here for?
You don't want me to be here?

28

Shhhh.

Don't shhhhhs me.

Listen I got some nice people in here.

I don't care about your nice people, I'm nice as anybody in town.

Where'd you get drunk at?

Everywhere, and who don't like me?

Well, you go right on back to where you got drunk at 'cause if you
stay here I'm gonna get you told.

Ain't nothin' you can tell me hot mama.

It look like you tryin' to take advantage of me, old gal from the
south.

Huh.

Every time I get a dance you come on up here and try to turn it out.

No I don't.

And you go on down and get your friend Patty Brown. You know
who I'm talkin' 'bout.

Sure.

And she don't do nothin' but lower my friends down to the ground.

Well, I'll tell you the reason why I do it Mrs. Lucy Ann.

Why?

'Cause you so dirty it look like you tryin' take everybody's man.

Now that's a lie. Come on now, get on up out of that chair.

For what?

Where you go from here honey, you know I really don't care.

Me neither.

This stanza sung: Just so you take it on out of here.

Before I hit you in the head with this chair.

Now don't be here when my pimp arrives,

what I'll put on you gal you will be surprised.

Now if you don't go, you'll wish you had a whip.

I'm gonna bust this dump because I've come to pay rent.

Now, take it on out of here, hot mama, I don't want you here.

How come you don't want me here.

Now the reason I don't want you here, you so doggone cheap.

Cheap?!

You bum one half pint of liquor and then you want to park a week.

That's what you say.

Now you been bummin' for six months, nothin' but liquor and beer.

Now you can tell, hot mama, the reason I don't want you here.

Yes, you sell that old no good whiskey.

What no good liquor?

And that ole rotten beer.

I made that still myself.

Well, chile, when I get through snitchin' on ya, huh, police are
gonna move ya from here.

Oh, ya gonna step on me.

You can go next door and talk about me to Elizabeth.

Ain't nobody tell you that.

And I'm scoot some snuff through your keyhole and make you
sneeze yourself to death.

Yes, honey, if you ever start to pimpin' on me, I got somethin' I'll do.

What is it?

I'll give you one more drink of my liquor and you know it's my high
brew.

That's what you think.

Honey, I got somethin' right here that shoots ninety-nine times.

What is it?

And when the first shot hits you, baby, you gonna change your
snitchin' mind.

Sung: Now take it on outa here, take it on outa here.

——Margaret Carter——

Biographical information about Margaret Carter, such as her birth date, death date and aliases, is not readily available. It is known, however, that Carter recorded the following songs, "Come Get Me Papa Before I Faint" and "I Want Plenty of Grease in My Fryin' Pan" in August of 1926 on Pathé Actuelle, in New York City (Dixon & Godrich).

Many of Carter's songs discuss the typical issues for a woman blues singer revealed previously in the Introduction. The lonesomeness a woman feels when her man rambles and the pain she feels when he does come home are the main subjects for "Come Get Me Papa Before I Faint." Carter explains her confusion, "I work hard all day for you, and I don't like the way you do." Even though she doesn't like the way he treats her, she doesn't know what to do with herself when he is gone, "You threw me down with no complaints, come on and get me papa before I faint."

From her song "I Want Plenty of Grease in My Fryin' Pan," one could make the assumption that she sang on the vaudeville circuit, as this song masks the discussion of sex by the frying pan metaphor. The frying pan represents her vagina and she illuminates her lover's insensitivity by stating, "I need plenty of grease in my frying pan 'cause I don't want my meat to burn," meaning that she needs to be ready for intercourse so that it won't hurt her. Thus, this song becomes a plea for her lover to understand sexuality from a woman's point of view.

"Come Get Me Papa, Before I Faint"

I've been blue most every day,
Ever since you been away,
I been thinking just of you and I want you, yes, I do.

I've been cravin' for your love,
True as all the stars above,
And you are always what I crave, that's why I'm gonna rave.
Come on and get me papa, before I faint.
Don't think I'm a jokin', 'cause I ain't.
I work hard all day for you, and I don't like the way you do.
Don't start to messing around with me, cause I've been as good as any
  gal could be.
You threw me down with no complaints, come on and get me before
  I faint.

Come on and get me papa, before I faint.
Don't think I'm a jokin', 'cause I ain't.
I work hard all day for you, and I don't like the way you do.
Don't start to messing around with me, cause I've been as good as any
  gal could be.
You threw me down with no complaints, come on and get me before
  I faint.

"I Want Plenty of Grease in My Fryin' Pan"

Peter Street from New Orleans, he's the laziest man I ever seen.
I was washin' hard in my back yard and I happened to get some love.
He made me so God darn mad and I screamed it all day.
He knew I could not fry my meat without lard,
And this is what I said.
I need plenty of grease in my fryin' pan 'cause I don't want my meat
  to burn.

You know I asked you once to give me some lard, but it seems that
  you cannot learn.
You know I use plenty a grease every day, but I ain't done no fryin'
  since you was away.
I need plenty of grease in my fryin' pan 'cause I don't want my meat
  to burn.

I need plenty of grease in my fryin' pan 'cause I don't want my meat
  to burn.

You know I asked you once to give me some lard, but it seems that
you cannot learn.
My fryin' pan was on the stove, gettin' hot,
I said sweet papa put some grease in my pot.
I need plenty of grease in my fryin' pan 'cause I don't want my meat
to burn.

Ida Cox

Ida Cox was born on February 25, 1896, in Toccoa, Georgia, and died November 10, 1967, in Knoxville, Tennessee (Harris). As a child, Ida Cox was an active participant in the choir in the African Methodist Church (Carr, Fairweather & Priestly). During her teenage years, Cox toured with minstrel shows and later she became active in the vaudeville circuit (Harris). Cox married the pianist and organist Jesse Crump (Feather).

The style of Cox's music is more typical of women's blues than is that of more overt singers like Lucille Bogan because Cox's language is clean and sexual activity is only referred to by using parallels or analogies. Cox's career in music forced her to leave home and travel. Because of this fact, Cox was forced to grow up quickly, and many of her songs reveal her understanding and perceptions of the world around her. While some of her songs contain advice such as in "Four Day Creep," which states, "When you lose your money, don't lose your mind," others reveal the harsh realities of the world that affect her and can only be alleviated by whiskey or moonshine. Many of Cox's songs contain elements of homesickness, as in her song "Cold and Blue," in which she says, "I cried all night like I never cried before, even father and mother had drove me from their door." Here, Cox may be making a reference to her leaving home when she was still quite young to make a career in music.

"Blues Ain't Nothin' But"

Rampart Street in New Orleans town,
Don't claim no one for miles around.
For Creoles it's it, I'm melting fast.
That's the best spot in all the land.

(They must have) a cabaret.
They play night into day.
I'm blue from my head down to my feet,
for good ole Rampart Street.

I'm first to go down to torment at sunset.
I want to hear that colored jazz band play.
The Cadillac, the Red Onion too,
good little boy and the park bench too.
You can enjoy yourself, down on Rampart Street.

I'm going to go down to torment at sunset.
I want to hear that colored jazz band play.
The Cadillac, the Red Onion too,
good little boy and the park bench too.
You can enjoy yourself, down on Rampart Street.

"Chattanooga Blues"

Climbed aboard Lookout Mountain, looked as far as I can see.
Tryin' to find a man that made a monkey outa me.
Race the devil in time to catch the cannonball.
Got the blues for Chattanooga, won't be back till late next fall.

Down in ticket market, (thought I went bust).
Ramblin' bunch a soldiers like you ever saw.
On the Tennessee River, down to the rocky dam,
I'm sittin' (on a good hard redwood), tryin' to find my good man Sam.

I was market to my callers, each man seen.
Watchin' everybody that I chanced to meet.
At last I found my daddy, (to my surprise).
Dressed in a tailor made suit and a brand new Stetson hat.

Daddy, sweet daddy, I know you quit me now,
'Cause I don't need no daddy no how.
'Cause trouble, trouble is all I ever find.
I'm goin' away, got to wear you off of my mind.

Down in Chattanooga, there's hospitality.
The finest bunch of people in the state of Tennessee.
Tired, tired of roaming this way.
Got the blues for Chattanooga, I'm going back to stay someday.

"Chicago Monkey Man"

I'm goin' to Chicago, darn, but I can't take you.
I'm goin' to Chicago, darn, but I can't take you.
'Cause there's nothin' there baby, that a monkey man can do.

I've got a monkey man here, a monkey man over there.
I've got a monkey man here, a monkey man over there.
If monkeys could be money, I'd be a Chicago millionaire.

I've got fourteen men now, and only want one more.
I've got fourteen men now, and only want one more.
And as soon as I get that one, I'll let these fourteen go.

Lord, I'm gonna tell you like the Dago told the Jew.
Lord, I'm gonna tell you like the Dago told the Jew.
When you no gotty no money, mommy can no longer usey you.

I can take my monkey men and set them all in line.
I can take my monkey men and set them all in line.
Anyone can count them three, four, five, seven, eight, nine.

"Blues Ain't Nothin' Else But"

Oh, the blues ain't nothin' but your lover on your mind.
Oh, the blues ain't nothin' but your lover on your mind.
The man that keeps you worryin' and always cryin'.

Oh, the blues ain't nothin' but a good woman wanting to see her man.
Oh, the blues ain't nothin' but a good woman wanting to see her man.
Can't get him when she wants him, got to get him when she can.

Oh, the blues ain't nothin but a slow achin' heart disease.
Oh, the blues ain't nothin but a slow achin' heart disease.
Just like consumption, it kills you by degree.

Oh, the blues ain't nothin' but a woman that cries night and day.
Oh, the blues ain't nothin' but a woman that cries night and day.
Cryin' about her lover another woman took away.

Oh, papa, papa, papa, mama's done gone mad.
Oh, papa, papa, papa, mama's done gone mad.
Oh, the blues ain't nothin' but a good woman feelin' bad.

"How Can I Miss You When I've Got Dead Aim?"

Don't let your man know he can make you blue.
'Cause if you do he'll make a fool outta you.
How can you miss him, honey, when you've got dead aim?

When one man won't, another one will.
But don't stop, girls, until you get your fill.
How can you miss him, honey, when you've got dead aim?

If your man quits you don't you wear no black.
Find the gal that ditched you for him and fight her back.
How can you miss him, honey, when you've got dead aim?

If you kill my dog, I'm gonna kill your cat.
I'm getting even with the world and there's nothing to that.
How can I miss him, honey, when I've got dead aim?

I've got a man in Georgia, a man in Tennessee.
But the Chicago man has put the thing on me.
How can I miss him, honey, when I've got dead aim?

The barhand clappers are all the rage,
But good women and good whiskey improve with age.
How can I miss him, honey, when I've got dead aim?

They say the blues is a habit that eats like rust.
Join the blue Monday crowds and play safety first.
How can you miss him, honey, when you've got dead aim?

"One Time Women Blues"

Some barhand clapper came and stole my man away.
Some barhand clapper came and stole my man away.
He's been gone two years but it seems to me like yesterday.

I'll get me a cannon, pistol, and a submarine.
I'll get me a cannon, pistol, and a submarine.
And go down to every man's house and treat the one time woman me.

I'm gonna lay in bed, if my face hangs to the wall,
I'm gonna lay in bed, if my face hangs to the wall,
And I'm gonna hangover, till I hear my daddy call.

One of these mornings' he's goin' to wake up almost dead.
One of these mornings' he's goin' to wake up almost dead.
And the doctor will be makin' stitches all across his head.

But here is something that he don't seem to understand.
But here is something that he don't seem to understand.
I'm a one time woman and I don't want no two time man.

"How Long, Daddy, How Long"

How long, how long, has that love bound train been gone?
How long, how long, baby, how long?

I feel like ramblin' (if you do too, then come on).
How long, how long, daddy, how long?

I've got the blues so bad I've got boxcars on my mind.
How long, how long, baby, how long?

I can't see my baby and it ain't no use in cryin'.
How long, how long, daddy, how long?

It takes a big engine to pull a fast man's train.
How long, how long, daddy, how long?

It takes a brown skinned man to run a woman insane.
How long, how long, daddy, how long?

How long, how long, daddy, do I have to wait.
How long, how long, baby, how long?

Can I get it now or do I have to hesitate?
How long, how long, daddy, how long?

"Pleading Blues"
(First stanza only is spoken)

Well girls, you know how you feel when your best man has quit you? And
   that's the case with me. And I want you to listen while I sing this song.
   And try and sympathize with me.

Sung: I've been worried night and day.
Since my daddy went away.
Do Lord, send him back to me.

Now, I can't stand to lose that man.
'Cause he's the sweetest man in the land.
Lordy, won't you hear my plea.

Now I can't help but sigh.
I can't help but cry.
Daddy please come back to me.
'Cause I'm blue as I can be.
Even though I miss you, you're the one and all I crave.
And you got a brand of lovin', daddy, really won't behave.

Tell me why you stayin' so long?
Don't you know you're doin' me wrong?
Just because I love you, you know that I'm not blind.
And if you call that quitting, get your way and (I'll start cryin').

'Cause I'm almost choked in pain and if you're the one to blame,
To tell the truth, sweet daddy, I should have let you be.
I wouldn't feel like cryin if you hadn't put that thing on me.

"Seven Day"

Every Monday mornin', people just whine (all) day.
Every Monday mornin', people just whine (all) day.
I think about my daddy, who's many miles away.

Every Tuesday mornin', whiskey is all I crave.
Every Tuesday mornin', whiskey is all I crave.
The blues and booze are gonna carry me to my grave.

Wednesday and Thursday, I try to wear the blues away.
Wednesday and Thursday, I try to wear the blues away.
But when you get 'em about your daddy, they really come to stay.

Every Friday people, is always my bad luck day.
Every Friday people, is always my bad luck day.
That's the day my man packed up and went away.

I woke up Saturday mornin', trying to find my man.
I woke up Saturday mornin', trying to find my man.
But I ain't got nobody to lend me a helping hand.

"Cold and Blue"

My daddy put me out last night in the rain and snow.
My daddy put me out last night in the rain and snow.
I was cold and blue, didn't have no place to go.

Top of my pillow, I slept on the frozen ground.
Top of my pillow, I slept on the frozen ground.
It was the only place I had to lay my weary body down.

I cried all night like I never cried before.
I cried all night like I never cried before.
Even father and mother had drove me from their door.

I felt like I was in some lion's den.
I felt like I was in some lion's den.
My man he mistreated me but he's sure, Lord, to sin again.

"Booze Crazy Man"

Daddy, oh sweet daddy, please don't drive me away.
Daddy, oh sweet daddy, please don't drive me away.
I love you, sweet papa, please let your mama stay.

Don't let your whiskey drive away your only friend.
Don't let your whiskey drive away your only friend.
You know I stuck with you, sweet daddy, through thick and thin.

I worked so hard for you, till mornin' I was almost dead.
I worked so hard for you, till mornin' I was almost dead.
Just for daddy to have some place to hang his weary head.

But now, I'm bein' treated like a slave.
But now, I'm bein' treated like a slave.
You're gonna let that whiskey carry you to your grave.

"Broadcasting"

Mr. Radio Announcer, please listen to my plea.
Mr. Radio Announcer, please listen to my plea.
Tune in on your radio and find my man for me.

I think you might find him walkin' down some lonely road.
I think you might find him walkin' down some lonely road.
Please call him for me, ruin my heart his heavy load.

Call every station, call every ship at sea.
Call every station, call every ship at sea.
'Cause I'll give the world to get him back to me.

I walk the floor till I've worn out all my shoes.
I walk the floor till I've worn out all my shoes.
Announce to the world, I've got those broadcasting blues.

"Fogyism"

Why do people believe in some old signs?
Why do people believe in some old signs?
To hear a hoodoo holler, someone is surely dyin'.

Some will break a mirror, cry about bad luck for seven years.
Some will break a mirror, cry about bad luck for seven years.
And if a black cat crosses them, they'll break right down in tears.

To dream of muddy water, trouble's knockin' at your door.
To dream of muddy water, trouble is knockin' at your door.
Your man is sure to leave you and never return no more.

When your man come home evil, tells you you are getting old.
When your man come home evil, tells you you are getting old.
That's a sure sign he's got someone else bakin' his jelly roll.

"Four Day Creep"

When you lose your money, don't lose your mind.
When you lose your money, don't lose your mind.
When you lose your good man, please don't mess with mine.

And I'm gonna buy me a bulldog, to watch my man while he sleeps.
I'm gonna buy me a bulldog, to watch my man while he sleeps.
Men are so doggone crooked, afraid he might make a four day creep.

Girls, I'm gonna tell you this, ain't gonna tell you nothin' else.
Girls, I'm gonna tell you this, ain't gonna tell you nothin' else.
Any woman's a fool to think she's got a whole man by herself.

But if you got a good man, and don't want him taken away from you,
Girls if you got a good man, and don't want him taken away from you,
Don't ever tell your friend woman, what your man can do.

Lord, Lord, I'm getting up and leave.
Lordy, Lordy, Lordy, I'm getting up and leave.
But mama ain't too old to shift her gears.

And I'm a big fat mama got some meat shakin' on my bones.
I'm a big fat mama got some meat shakin' on my bones.
And every time I shake, some skinny gal loses her home.

——— Mary Dixon———

Mary Dixon's "Daddy, You've Got Everything" was recorded on Wednesday, March 20, 1929, on Columbia label in New York City. This song praises a man who knows well how to satisfy a woman. Many references to sex such as, "Make me throw my hands up high, feels so good I want to die" and "When I'm feeling awful blue, daddy, nothin' I won't do" are made throughout the song, although they are covered with clean language, probably so as not to offend a theater audience.

"Daddy, You've Got Everything" expresses a rare occasion when a woman is content with a man; it is an unusual blues song in that it does not portray an atmosphere of misery or melancholy. Even the tune to this song is upbeat in tempo and the lyrics harbor no complaint. Rather, in this song, a woman relishes her happiness and glorifies the man in her life.

"Daddy, You've Got Everything"

Take me daddy, on your knee, tell me what you think of me.
Hug me papa, till I frown, make my kindness tumble down.
Daddy, you've got everything.

Make me throw my hands up high, feels so good I want to die.
Take your time with what you do, make me cry for more of you.
Mmmm, daddy, you've got everything.

When I'm feeling awful blue, daddy, nothin' I won't do.
There ain't nothin' I can't stand, I'm as much woman as you
    are man.
Daddy, you've got everything.

Kiss me till I feel the same, make me want to shake that thing.
Give me everything and how, if you are a man then show it now.
Daddy, you've got everything.

Honey we can dim the lights, make believe we were tonight.
Oh, run your hand all through my hair, mmm, the sky's the limit
    and I don't care.
Daddy, you've got everything.
I mean everything.

Lizzie Douglas
— (Memphis Minnie) —

Lizzie Douglas, better known as Memphis Minnie, and also as Kid, Gospel Minnie, Minnie McCoy, Minnie, or Texas Tessie, was born on June 3, 1897, in Algiers, Louisiana, and died August 6, 1973 (Harris). Memphis Minnie was one of thirteen children (Harris), which may have contributed to her running away from home to start a career in music at an early age.

Unlike many of her peers, Memphis Minnie was an excellent guitar player, and many of her songs are accompanied by her on guitar. One of her most popular songs is entitled "Ain't Nothin' in Ramblin'," and it may be that Memphis Minnie wrote this song as a response to having left home at such an early age to pursue her musical career, as the song criticizes and condemns the notion of rambling as a whole.

Aside from her guitar playing expertise, Memphis Minnie can easily be recognized by her high pitched howls occurring in the middle of her songs. For example, in "Jockey Man Blues" the word "pleasin'" is drawn out and sung in a variety of pitches the same way the word "woopee" is carried out in "I'm Waitin' on You." Minnie is also known for her use of nonsense words like "mmmmmmm" that function to portray the singer's misery in the midst of the blues song. Minnie's "Ma Rainey" is a classic example of the use of such sounds.

"Frankie Jean"

One time my papa had a hog.
His name was Frank Jean.

45

Man that's the meanest hog the world ever seen.
Ain't it just do me good to ride on Frank Jean.

And it do you good to sit and listen to him
Sometime when he comin' down that pike road.
Almost make his feet talk.
Man that craziest hog the world has ever seen.
Somethin' kinda like this.
Go on, Frank Jean go on.

I had him out with me once, he got loose.
I couldn't catch him to save my life.
I called Frankie Jean and I called him.
He didn't seem to pay me no mind.
I told my papa, "How do you do to catch a hog?"
He said, "How did you do it?"
I said, "I called mine."
Frankie Jean, I called him. He didn't pay me no attention.
That's a hog, you didn't call him right.
You gotta whistle when you want a hog to come to ya.
Somethin' kinda like this.
(whistles)
Then he'll come and straight to me.
So I took him out again, he got loose from me.
I called him and called him.
He didn't seem to pay me no attention.
I thought about what papa said.
You's a hog. I must whistle for you.
Somethin' like this.
(whistles)
Then he comin' and straight to me.
I had him on the ranch once.
I had five thousand dollars bettin' on Frank Jean.
Folks, I wasn't scared at all.
'Cause I know he wouldn't let me lose.
For if he let me lose, he'd run off all his shoes.
Somethin' like this.
Go on Frankie.

"Preacher's Blues"

Some folks say a preacher won't steal.
I caught three in my cornfield.
One had a yellow, one had a brown.
Looked over in the middle, one was gettin' down.
Some folks say that a preacher won't steal.
But if I do my stealin' then I get regular meals.

I went to my house, 'bout half past ten.
Looked over at my bed to where that preacher had been.
Now, some folks say that a preacher won't steal.
But if I do my stealin' then I get regular meals.

They will eat your chicken, they will eat your pie.
They will eat your wife out on the sly.
Now, some folks say that a preacher won't steal.
But if I do my stealin' then I get regular meals.

I been tryin' so hard, tryin' to save my life,
Tryin' to keep that preacher from my wife.
Now, some folks say that a preacher won't steal.
But if I do my stealin' then I get regular meals.

I went out last night, came in late,
I found out where you made a date.
Now, some folks say that a preacher won't steal.
But if I do my stealin' then I get regular meals.

And I told you once, done told you twice.
Look after that preacher or he will love your wife.
Now, some folks say a preacher won't steal.
But if I do my stealin' then I get regular meals.

"If You See My Rooster"

If you see my rooster, please run him on back home.
If you see my rooster, please run him on back home.
I haven't found eggs laid in my basket, since my rooster been gone.

I heard my rooster crowing this morning just about the break
of day.

I heard my rooster crowing this morning just about the break
   of day.
I guess that's just about the time he was draggin' his hen away.

I just found him, a comin' this a way.
I just found him, a comin' this a way.
Every time I look around, my rooster's goin' away.

I've got too many hens out in my yard, can't keep no rooster
   at home.
I've got too many hens out in my yard, can't keep no rooster
   at home.
I don't know what's the matter, but it's somethin' goin' on wrong,

Now if you see my rooster, please run him on back home.
Now if you see my rooster, please run him on back home.
Ain't found no eggs laid in my basket since my rooster been gone.

"Don't Bother It"

I know I'm good, I tried to be kind,
But that stuff I got you know it costs a lot of money.
Please don't bother it. Oh, don't bother it.
Oh, please don't bother it because it don't belong to me.

Ain't no use gettin' mad, standin' on your head,
After you're through with that thing it really will kill you dead.
Please don't bother it. Oh, don't bother it.
Oh, please don't bother it because it don't belong to me.

Now listen here, baby, I don't want to make you mad.
I don't want you to bother somethin' that you ain't never had.
Please don't bother it. Oh, don't bother it.
Oh, please don't bother it because it don't belong to me.

I done told you once, I done told you twice,
After you get through with that thing you really will lose your life.
Please don't bother it. Oh, don't bother it.
Oh, please don't bother it because it don't belong to me.

I know the night watchman, he keeps me here today.
Just to keep your boys from stealin' that thing away.

Please don't bother it. Oh, don't bother it.
Oh, please don't bother it because it don't belong to me.

And I hate to see you gettin' dry.
Takin' over somethin' that your money really cannot buy.
Please don't bother it. Oh, don't bother it.
Oh, please don't bother it because it don't belong to me.
Leave it alone.

"Today, Today Blues"

Lord, today, today, today, today,
Lord, today, today, today, today,
I'm gonna catch me a train and ride my blues away.

Come here, baby, and look me in my eye.
Come here, baby, and look me in my eye.
You know the troubles I'm havin', I am bound to die.

Today, today, oh, today, today.
Today, today, oh, today, today.
I'm gonna catch me a train and ride my blues away.

If you ever quit me, baby, I wouldn't do you no harm.
If you ever quit me, baby, I wouldn't do you no harm.
I would just get me another man and I would go ahead on.

Today, today, oh, today, today.
Today, today, oh, today, today.
I'm gonna catch me a train and ride my blues away.

"Socket Blues"

Down in my own home town, the pot's on the stove but I've got to
    have a socket everywhere I go.
I need a socket, oh I need a socket, babe, I've got to have a socket if
    you want me to iron your clothes.

I got your clothes on the ground, I can't find no socket around.
I need a socket, oh I need a socket, babe I need a socket if you want
    me to iron your clothes.

But I need a socket in my hand you got a lot of dough.
I don't know what you expect for me to iron your clothes.
I need a socket, oh I need a socket, babe, I need a socket if you want
    me to iron your clothes.

Well the reason I love my baby, I love him so,
He carries me a socket everywhere I go.
I need a socket, oh I need a socket, babe, I've got to have a socket if
    you want me to iron your clothes.

I got a liquid iron, I got plenty of steam,
But a socket now is really all I need.
I need a socket, oh I need a socket, babe, I need a socket if you want
    me to iron your clothes.

"When You're Asleep"

When you're asleep, I mean dead asleep,
You shoulda known what's goin' on wrong.
When you're awoke, walk around on your feet,
You shoulda known what's goin' on wrong.

When you're sick, sick down in your bed,
You shoulda known what's goin' on wrong.
When you're not sick, walkin' round on your feet,
You shoulda known what's goin' on wrong.

I'm glad, I'm not sad, I'm pleased that I'm never mad.
Lord, I shoulda known what's goin' on wrong.

If you are blind, blind you cannot see,
You shoulda known what's goin' on wrong.
If you're not blind, walkin' round on your feet,
You shoulda known what's goin on wrong.

If you're in trouble, I mean in trouble,
You shoulda known what's goin' on wrong.
But if you're not in trouble, up walkin' round on your feet,
You shoulda known what's goin' on wrong.

I'm glad, I'm not sad, I'm pleased I'm never mad.
Lord, I shoulda known what's goin' on wrong.

"Jockey Man Blues"

Good mornin', blues, please shake hands with me.
Good mornin', blues, please shake hands with me.
I've got the blues this mornin', just as low as I can be.

How can I sleep nights baby, when you turn your back on me?
How can I sleep nights baby, when you turn your back on me?
I'm gonna take my troubles go on down by the sea.

You can eat in my kitchen, sleep in my bed, 'fore I'm old, pretty
    papa, rest your weary head.
'Cause I need, need some lovin' now.
I haven't had no one to love me like you know how.

I woke up this mornin' with the risin' sun.
I woke up this mornin' with the risin' sun.
My pretty papa's a jockey and he sure don't ride for fun.

If you see my jockey, I say, please tell him hurry home.
If you see my jockey, I say, please tell him hurry home.
I ain't had no lovin', Lord, since my jockey been gone.

My guy wrote this mornin' and my love come fallin' down.
My guy wrote this mornin' and my love come fallin' down.
I'll be your monkey woman but please don't lead me around.

Take a race horse runnin', a jockey ride around.
Take a pretty seal skin, papa, make my love come down.
'Cause I don't feel welcome pleasin' by myself.
Lord, since you run away and left me, I don't want nobody else.

"I'm Waitin' on You"

I met a boy, he's only twelve years old,
I want to take him home with me.

Everybody's tellin me that I was too old,
But I'll wait, darlin,' don't you see.
I'm waitin', oh, don't you see,
I'm waitin' on you, tell me you're waitin' on me.
I'm waitin', oh, don't you see,
I'm waitin' on you, tell me you're waitin' on me.

'Cause I don't mean to be so bold,
Just want to get you told,
I'll be tidyin' up all a my clothes,
Then says you don't want to go.
'Cause blues sittin' here and I'm waitin', don't you see,
I'm waitin' on you, tell me you're waitin' on me.

I'm waitin', oh, don't you see, I'm waitin' on you, tell me you're
    waitin' on me.
I'm waitin', oh, don't you see, I'm waitin' on you, tell me you're
    waitin' on me.

'Cause I may be treatin' you right, don't sleep with me at night.
And if you mess around here in my sight,
tell you boy, say it's quite all right.
'Cause blues sittin' here and I'm waitin', don't you see,
I'm waitin' on you, tell me you're waitin' on me.

"Keep On Goin'"

I beg you baby, treat me right.
You don't do nothin' but fuss and fight.
So now you keep on a goin', oh, keep on goin',
Now you can keep on goin', honey, 'til I change my mind.

You get away from my window; quit hangin' round my door.
I got another man, I don't want you no more.
So, now you keep on a goin', oh, keep on goin',
So, now you can keep on goin', honey, till I change my mind.

Now you needn't come a runnin', holdin' up your hands.
You go to your woman, I got me another man.
So now you keep on a goin', oh, keep on goin',
Now you can keep on goin', honey, till I change my mind.

I might tell you a little somethin', don't aim to make you mad.
But it's good to have somethin' that you never had.
So now you keep on a goin', oh, keep on goin',
Now you can keep on goin', honey, till I change my mind.

When I had you baby, you know you wouldn't treat me right.
You take my money, stay away from me at night.
So you keep on a goin', oh, keep on goin',
So you can keep on goin', honey, till I change my mind.

"I'm a Gamblin' Woman"

I'm a gamblin' woman, gamble everywhere I go.
I'm a gamblin' woman, gamble everywhere I go.
I've lost so much money, bettin' the dice on 5, 10, 4.

I've got me a mojo, for as I can't lose no more.
Yes, I've got me a mojo, for as I can't lose no more.
Well, you know you can't beat me, I've got to win everywhere I go.

I gambled all last night, all last night before.
I gambled all last night, all last night before.
I win so much money, I start to take back my mojo.

I shot crap all last night until the break of day.
I shot crap all last night until the break of day.
I been haulin' in all that pretty money, and that market man had to
    run away.

Mmmmmmm, Got me a three on twelve.
Mmmmmmm, Got me a three on twelve.
If you roll seven eleven, this mojo can go to hell.

"I'm a Bad Luck Woman"

Every man I get if he don't get sick he will die.
Don't some other woman take him like on the doggone fly.
I'm a bad luck woman, I'm a bad luck woman, I'm a bad luck woman,
    I can't see the reason why.

Well, the next one I got you know he works very hard.
Just as soon as I got him in love he lost his doggone job.
I'm a bad luck woman, I'm a bad luck woman, I'm a bad luck woman,
  I can't see the reason why.

Well, the next man I got he was a railroad man.
Just as soon as I got him he took everything that I doggone had.
I'm a bad luck woman, I'm a bad luck woman, I'm a bad luck woman,
  I can't see the reason why.

Well, the next man I got he was long and tall.
Every time I look around he's kickin' in some other man's stall.
I'm a bad luck woman, I'm a bad luck woman, I'm a bad luck woman,
  I can't see the reason why.

Well, the next man I got he was short and fat.
I couldn't keep him because he wasn't tight like that.
I'm a bad luck woman, I'm a bad luck woman, I'm a bad luck woman,
  I can't see the reason why.

Well, the next man I got was a fat hog in his seat.
I had him two days and he got drawn away from me.
I'm a bad luck woman, I'm a bad luck woman, I'm a bad luck woman,
  I can't see the reason why.

Well, the next man I got bought me a hat and a dress.
And every time I look around the police had him on a doggone arrest.
I'm a bad luck woman, I'm a bad luck woman, I'm a bad luck woman,
  I can't see the reason why.

"Caught Me Wrong Again"

Well, you caught me, baby, we was makin' friends.
I can't say nothin' because I'm wrong again.
You caught me my daddy, we was makin' friends.
Well I can't say nothin', you caught me wrong again.

You know you're parked at my house and you can't get in.
That's the time you caught me and my baby makin' friends
When you come to my house and you can't get in.
Well I can't say nothin', you caught me wrong again.

If it hadn't a been for me my man would never been in pen.
Every time he look around he catch me makin' friends.
If it hadn't a been for me my man would not been in pen.
Now he got himself thrown in jail, he done caught his wife wrong
again.

You know when you give me that money go down town and pay that
bill you owe.
I take that money and buy my man a suit of clothes.
'Cause I was just tryin' to make friends, yes, I'm makin' friends.
Well I can't say nothin', you caught me wrong again.

Now if I give you my money you better not run around.
If you got that in your mind you better lay my money down.
Lord, don't try to make friends, yes, you makin' friends,
Well you can't say nothin, your wife just caught you wrong again.

"Livin' the Best I Can"

Everybody's talkin' 'bout how I'm livin', but I'm livin' the best I can.
Everybody's talkin' 'bout how I'm livin', but I'm livin' the best I can.
I got a man who stays in the shade, I'm tryin' to work to make this
grade.
Everybody's talkin' 'bout how I'm livin', but I'm givin' it the best I
can.

Everybody's talkin' 'bout how I'm livin', but I'm livin' the best I can.
Everybody's talkin' 'bout how I'm livin', but I'm livin' the best I can.
When you see me up around about four, down on my knees
scrubbin' somebody's floor.
Everybody's talkin' 'bout how I'm livin', but I'm givin' it the best I
can.

Everybody's talkin' 'bout how I'm livin', but I'm livin' the best I can.
Everybody's talkin' 'bout how I'm livin', but I'm livin' the best I can.
When you see me up around about six, tryin' to get my dinner fixed.
Everybody's talkin' 'bout how I'm livin', but I'm givin' it the best I
can.

Everybody's talkin' 'bout how I'm livin', but I'm livin' the best I can.
Everybody's talkin' 'bout how I'm livin', but I'm livin' the best I can.

I don't think I'm doin' so bad, I've got the same man now I've always had.

Everybody's talkin' 'bout how I'm livin', but I'm givin' it the best I can.

I mean, givin' it the best I can.

"No Need You Doggin' Me"

Ain't no need you doggin' me when I ain't done nothin' to you.
I ain't done nothin' to you.
Well, if you keep doggin' me, ain't no tellin' what I may do.

Well, you dog me every mornin' and you dog me late at night.
You dog me late at night.
If you keep doggin' me, how you expect me to treat you right?

Well, I'm goin' away to leave you, who you gonna dog when I'm gone?
Who you gonna dog when I'm gone?
Well, I know it's gonna be lonesome but I can't see no peace at home.

I'm went to the station and my train had just gone.
My train had just gone.
I'm gonna leave tell my soul, I've got to take your doggin' ways right on.

Here I go with my bottle up under my arm.
With my bottle up under my arm.
I was just a little too late, my train had done been here and gone.

"I'm Going Don't You Know"

Turn that steak down, don't you know?
You are goin' let me hear you blow.
Hey, hey, hey hey, everybody's goin'. Yes, I'm goin' don't you know?

Everybody's got their chicken, where's mine?
Look like to me I'm gonna be left behind.
Hey, hey, hey hey, everybody's goin'. Yes, I'm goin' don't you know?

Now, go home and pack up everything you got.
Be real afraid of that run down clock.
Hey, hey, hey hey, everybody's goin'. Yes, I'm goin' don't you know?

Now, don't keep me waitin' on the corner so long.
Train at the station and she'll soon be gone.
Hey, hey, hey hey, everybody's goin' Yes, I'm goin' don't you know?

You done fooled around here and made me miss that train.
Now I've got to catch me an airplane.
Hey, hey, hey hey, everybody's goin' Yes, I'm goin' don't you know?

Well, everybody's goin', babe, and I want to go too.
Don't you hear me talkin that sweet talk to you?
Hey, hey, hey hey, everybody's goin'. Yes, I want to go too.

"Hustlin' Woman Blues"

I sit on the corner all night long,
Counting the stars one by one.
Sit on the corner all night long,
Counting the stars one by one.
I didn't make no money, oh and then I can't go back home.
Spoken: I got a bad man.

My man stops in the window with a .45 in his hand.
My man stops in the window with a .45 in his hand.
Every now and then he gets up and hollers at me, and tells me, "You
    better not miss that man."
Spoken: I got it baby.

My daddy ain't got no shoes, but now he's done got cold.
My daddy ain't got no shoes, but now he's done got cold.
I gonna grab me somebody, if I don't make me some dough.

Spoken: "I'm goin' to the carnival bar. Can you gamble? No, it's bad
    when you can't do nothin'. I just want to know, can you shoot
    the dice? No, can't shoot no dice. I can't gamble myself. But I
    can't do nothin'. But I bet a man that I can gamble."

I'm goin to the corner store, see what I can find.
I'm goin to the corner store, see what I can find.
And if I make a hundred dollars, I will bring my daddy ninety-nine.

"Ma Rainey"

I was thinkin' 'bout Ma Rainey, wonderin' where could Ma
  Rainey be.
I was thinkin' 'bout Ma Rainey, wonderin' where could Ma
  Rainey be.
I been lookin' for her, even down in Tennessee.

She was born in Georgia, travel all over this world.
She was born in Georgia, travel all over this world.
And she's the best blues singer, people, that I ever heard.

When she made "Bo-Weevil Blues," I was livin' way down in Lyons.
When she made "Bo-Weevil Blues," I was livin' way down in Lyons.
Every time I hear that record, I just couldn't keep from cryin'.

Mmmmmmm, Mmmmmmmmmm, Mmmmmmmmmmmmmm
Mmmmmmmm, Mmmmmmmmmmmm, Mmmmmmmmmmmmm,
Mmmmmmmm, Mmmmmmmmmmmm, poor Ma Rainey.

People sure live lonesome since Ma Rainey been gone.
People sure live lonesome since Ma Rainey been gone.
But she left Memphis Minnie, to carry her good works on.

——— Cleo Gibson ———

According to Dixon and Godrich, Cleo Gibson's given name was Cleoseohus, and she toured as half of a pair of vaudeville performers known as Gibson & Gibson. Her birth and death dates are not recorded in any known anthology or encyclopedia. Very few of her recordings exist today, but her performance of "I've Got Movements in My Hips" marks a valuable contribution to American blues music.

This song portrays the woman in comparison to a Ford engine, showing the well known American metaphor of woman as a car. When Gibson says, "Well, you know all about those machines, start a movement you ain't never seen," she is implicitly comparing the acceleration of a Packard to the accelerating movements that accompany intercourse. She later uses words such as "guaranteed" which remind us of warranties that are issued on cars. Gibson directly parallels herself with the Packard her boyfriend is so interested in, "My poor little car, everybody wants to ride, jump in, you will see," making herself marketable or desirable to the man she seeks. Hence, Gibson's performance of "I've Got Movements in My Hips" signifies an early appreciation of the woman as car metaphor that now appears in abundance.

"I've Got Movements in My Hips"

Now, listen kind folks, what I have to say, happened 'bout a
    week ago.
All about Valentina, my true lover's gone.
Valentina, he was smooth, quick as a Packard and stuff.
But lover Joe, was like a Ford, and a little bit too rough.

Well, you know all about these machines, start a movement you ain't
    never seen.
I got Ford engine movement in my hips, 10,000 miles guaranteed.
My poor little car, everybody wants to ride, jump in, you will see.
You can all have a Rolls Royce, your Packard and stuff, take an old
    engine, boys, to do your stuff.
I got more than the movements in my hips, 10,000 miles guaranteed.
I say, 10,000 miles guaranteed.

I got Ford engine movement in my hips, 10,000 miles guaranteed.
My poor little car, everybody wants to ride, jump in, you will see.
You can all have a Rolls Royce, your Packard and stuff, take an old
    engine, boys, to do your stuff.
I got Ford engine movements in my hips, 10,000 miles guaranteed.
I say, 10,000 miles guaranteed.

—— Lilian Goodner ——

Dixon and Godrich record what might possibly be all that is known about Lilian Goodner; they reveal that "Gonna Get Somebody's Daddy" was recorded in February 1924 by Goodner and her band, the "Sawin' Three."

Interestingly, Goodner recorded another song called "Four Flushin' Papa," wherein she chastises and threatens her lover for being unfaithful. In "Four Flushin' Papa," Goodner says:

> Lay your cards down on the table right where your mama can see,
>   where she can see.
> I'm the only queen you can have in your jack.
> If another queen's chosen she's sure to be a wreck.
> Four flushin' papa, you gotta play straight with me.

This sets up a double standard when compared to her words in "Gonna Get Somebody's Daddy:"

> I'm gonna rob somebody's daddy all alone, all alone in my home.

While Goodner expects her "four flushin' papa" to play straight with her, she boasts about becoming a paramour, saying that she is "gonna rob somebody's baby." This may illuminate once again the hierarchical struggles for black females of this era; while she may only threaten the man in her life about remaining faithful, she may exert power through sex by seducing a married man. This may give a woman an illusion of control in an otherwise powerless existence.

"Gonna Get Somebody's Daddy"

Now, look here Henry Thomson, spend some time on me.
Now I can make you do it, what you doin' to me.
I tried you once, I tried you twice, now I confess,
That you ain't a bit a different from the rest.
I've been a fool for you, now I'll tell you what I'm goin' to do.
I'm gonna get somebody's daddy for my own, for my own, for my own.
I'm gonna rob somebody's daddy all alone, all alone in my home.
I'm sick and tired of being lonely all the time, I'm bound to lose my mind.
Anytime a man stays out from home all night, walks right in and finds that everything's all right,
Starts to fighting me and starts to wreck my flat,
Say, what kind of a man is that?
Gonna get a man and find for him a brand new home.
Where he can do his fighting on a rented phone.
When if the chances are that he will let me be,
Daddy just wait and see.
Remember way last winter when the snow was deep,
you pawned your clothes and had me fixed right up complete.
You had most everything I had from coat to hat,
Then you hauled off and left me flat.
So now that I am lookin' good and on my feet,
And got another daddy who is nice and sweet,
You'll get a long vacation if you bother me,
Daddy just wait and see.

—— Rosa Henderson ——

Rosa Henderson — alias Flora Dale, Rosa Green, Mae Harris, Mamie Harris, Sara Johnson, Sally Ritz, Josephine Thomas, Gladys White, Bessie Williams — was born on November 24, 1896, in Henderson, Kentucky, and died on April 6, 1968, in New York, New York (Harris). The *Biographical Dictionary of Afro-American & African Musicians* reveals that Henderson began performing in 1913 in her uncle's tent show and expanded her career by actively participating in theatrical productions such as "The Harlem Rounders," "The Seventh Avenue Studlers," "Blackouts of 1929" and "Blackberries Revue" in Harlem theaters in the 1920s.

Rosa Henderson toured on the vaudeville circuit (Harris), and like many other female blues singers, she left home while still quite young to pursue her musical talents. Rosa Henderson's music is typical of the vaudeville style, as it closely conforms to the appropriate language expected of the vaudeville singers. For example, the song "Somebody's Doing What You Wouldn't Do" alludes to sex without mentioning sexual acts explicitly. Many of her other songs discuss relationships between males and females; however, Henderson's style is almost always reserved in manner.

"Somebody's Doing What You Wouldn't Do"

Oh, I came to say that I'm through.
I don't get any love from you.
I hope that this won't make you sad.

I say, our parting makes me glad.
Somebody's doin' just what you wouldn't do, just what you couldn't
    do, that's why I wasn't true.
Somebody's wooin' just like you couldn't woo.
Somebody weeps, somebody sleeps, somebody can't be beat.
And I'm getting lots of hurting, since I fell in love I won't be blue.
Somebody's kissing just like you wouldn't do.
That's why I'm through with you.

Somebody's doin' just like you wouldn't do, just what you couldn't
    do, that's why I wasn't true.
Somebody's wooin' just like you couldn't woo.
Somebody weeps, somebody sleeps, somebody can't be beat.
You're back fighting, out all-nighting.
And you're sliding don't make me blue.
Somebody's kissing just like you wouldn't do.
That's why I'm through with you.

Bertha Hill

Bertha Hill, also known as "Chippie" Hill, was born on March 15, 1905, in Charleston, South Carolina, and died on May 7, 1950, in New York, New York (Harris). According to Carr, Fairweather & Priestly, Hill sang with Ma Rainey and recorded with Louis Armstrong and Lonnie Johnson. *Jazz: The Essential Companion* also tells us that Hill sang at the Club Delisa in Chicago, the Village Vanguard in New York City and at Jimmy Ryan's at the Paris Jazz Fest.

Chippie Hill left home at the age of 14 to pursue her career in music; she was one of 16 children (Harris). She toured on the TOBA circuit of vaudeville (Harris), and was trained in a manner similar to that of her cohorts. Hill knew the famous Ma Rainey and according to Feather, she joined Rainey's show as a dancer and singer. She occasionally performed with Louis Armstrong and peaked in popularity in 1925 (Feather).

Like her peer Bessie Smith, Chippie Hill was killed in an automobile accident in the prime of her life. She died in a Harlem hospital (Harris); she might have lived had she been treated in a more adequately supplied white hospital. Hill recorded other songs not appearing in this anthology including "Mess Katie Mess" and "Lonesome All Alone and Blue."

"Street Walkin' Blues"
(All lines are spoken except the last four stanzas which are sung)

Who the devil is that down knockin' at my door?
(Man's voice): This is the landlord, I come here to collect my rent
    this mornin', ain't you got nothin' for me?
I'm sorry, Big Boy.

(Man's voice): You're sorry, and you always is sorry, and you ain't
never got nothin'. You been in my house six months and always
sorry.

I don't owe ya nothin' but five or six months little ole house rent.

(Man's voice): What kinda woman is that? How long you expect to
stay here? Five, six little ole weeks, months, years, Sundays and
everything and that ain't nothin', huh?

Well I can move.

(Man's voice): You can move but believe me you're gonna pay off
before you leave. Because if you don't I'm gonna have that
wagon up here, I mean and move you and everything, those
little babies and everything.

Sung: Got the street walkin' blues, when I walk the streets all night.
Got the street walkin' blues, walkin' straight through night and day.
I've gotta walk, I mean walk, until I walk these blues away.

Stood on the corner, till my feet are soakin' wet.
Stood on the corner, till my feet are soakin' wet.
Singin' the street walkin' blues, to each and every one I met.

Baby, if you ain't got a dollar, give me just one lousy dime.
If you ain't got a dollar, give me just one lousy dime.
'Cause the landlord's singin', just because my rent's behind.

I got the street walkin' blues, ain't gonna walk the streets no more.
Got the street walkin' blues, ain't gonna walk the streets no more.
('Cause the cops is gettin' bad, and the door is always closed.)

── Alberta Hunter ──

Alberta Hunter, alias May Alix, Josephine Beatty, Helen Roberts, was born on April 1, 1895, in Memphis, Tennessee (Harris), and died in 1984 (Herzhaft). Carr, Fairweather & Priestly divulge the interesting fact that Hunter retired from the blues scene in 1956 when she was 61 to become a nurse, but in 1977 she resumed her singing talent to sing at Barney Josephson's Cookery in New York City.

We know that Alberta Hunter sang the blues well into her old age, and unlike many of her cohorts, she witnessed progress in social reform for African Americans. Her voice is clear and crisp, and she often uses her voice to discuss elements of society which displease her. Her song "You Can't Tell the Difference After Dark" appears as a protest on the problems of racism, as she expresses the shallowness of individuals who like other people based on the color of their skin. In this song, which is upbeat in tempo, Hunter says, "I may be as brown as a berry, but that's only secondary. And you can't tell the difference after dark." Hunter speaks her mind, but does so in a way that does not evoke anger from racists; rather the pleasant tune of the song eases the words that may provoke hatred and misunderstanding from those in the prejudiced crowd. This song was not able to be included in this anthology.

"Second Hand Man"

Now it's a long, long story, but you want to hear it?
Say yes, 'cause I'm gonna tell it anyhow.
I've got a man trained to my hand
And I think I'm through huntin' now.

And what I'm tellin' you is private and I hope it will be kept that way.
No, he's not new, 'cause I'm number two, and that is why I say:
He's been used, but not abused, and I choose not to lose that second
   handed man o' mine.
Now he's kinda worn and he's slightly torn, and still I've sworn not
   to loan that second handed man o' mine.
Now you talk about promotions, that baby's made the grade and how.
He used to be, you know, just my extra man, ah, but he's on regular
   now.
He's kinda bold and he likes to scold, but folks, he brings salvation
   to my soul.
I'm talkin' 'bout that, 'bout that second handed man o' mine.
This man I'm talkin' bout' is like a pipe, you know, nice and ripe,
   yes in age, and he's just the type.
I'm talkin' 'bout that second handed man o' mine.
Now, he ain't no beaut, but he's kinda cute.
And he plays music, but not a flute.
And still I'm talkin' 'bout that second handed man o' mine.
Ah this baby's all the flavors, there ain't none after him.
'Cause I'm kinda fickle, 'cause I said the same thing when I met
   Sonny Jim.
Now he's not too fat, kinda tight like that.
And he's just like Babe Ruth at a bat.
I'm ravin' 'bout that second handed man o' mine.

"Send Me a Man"

Hanna Green from New Orleans, Hanna and her man had a terrible
   bout.
He packed up everything he had without a word and walked right
   out.
Hanna didn't weep, she didn't moan, not a tear ran down her face.
She just picked up the telephone and called the employment place.
She said, Send me a man that's not too fast and one that's not too
   slow.
Send me a man that you're sure can last until I say let go. Now I
   don't want no man that's gonna watch the clock, 'cause I've
   had plenty of that kind.

What I want is a man with an easy route and don't mind overtime.
And another thing, I don't want a man that's gonna weaken in the
    middle of a test.
What I want is a man that likes to tackle his job without always
    having to be asked, and then he can take his time. I don't want
    him to hurry.
This ain't no one night stand, so be sure to send me somebody that
    you know can really take it.
Please send me a man.
Send me a man that's not too rough and one that's not too nice.
I don't want no man that has to quit after he does a thing once or
    twice.
And another thing, I can't stand a man who plays around and when
    he says he's through, I got to go out and scout around and find
    somebody to finish up what he tried to do.
What I want is a man that knows when to tackle his job and when to
    let it be and I'd like to have a man that can use his head, in case
    of emergencies.
I don't want a man with just one stroke; I detest the same old brand.
    What I crave is something unusual. Please send me a man.

"I'll See You Go"

Say you're growin' tired of me, that you found somebody new.
But you'll never find another with a love like mine for you.
Remember these words, you'll want me back someday.

Well I share your every heartache, every burden I helped you share.
When you needed consolation, I have always been right there.
I was your friend, now you mistreat poor me.

When the person that you trusted has turned her back on you;
When you're broke, blue and disgusted, and you don't know what
    to do;
You can call on me, babe, I'll see you go.

When misfortune overtakes you and your youth and charm have gone;
When your fair weather friends forsake you, Lord, I'll still be hangin'
    on.
You're on top now, and you can't see poor me.

But here's one thing you should remember and it come to pass before;
It is written down in the good Book, you got to reap just what you
    sow.
And when it comes to you, babe, I'll see you go.

"Fine and Mellow"

My man don't love me, he treats me awfully mean.
Lord, my man don't love me, he treats me awfully mean.
He's about the lowest viper I ever seen.

He wears high draped pants, stripes are really yellow.
He wears high draped pants, stripes are really yellow.
But when he starts in to love me, he's so fine and mellow.

Love will make you drink and gamble, stay out all night long.
Love will make you drink and gamble, stay out all night long.
Love will make you do things that you know are wrong.

If you treat me right, baby, I'll stay home every day.
If you treat me right, daddy, I'll stay home every day.
But if you treat me wrong, baby, you're gonna drive me away.

Love is just like faucet, it turns off and on.
Love is just like faucet, it turns off and on.
Sometimes when you think it's on, babe, it's turned off and gone.

"Yelpin' the Blues"

I'll stand in my back door and yelp the blues all day.
I can stand in my back door and yelp the blues all day.
I can see the man that leads my poor mind astray.

My man was built like Gable, had a face just like a hog.
My man was built like Gable, had a face just like a hog.
He was a dirty no gooder and he treated me just like a dog.

Did you ever wake up with the blues all around your bed?
Did you ever wake up with the blues all around your bed?
And you didn't have a human being to hold your achin' head.

As sure as there's a heaven and as sure the stars do shine,
Just as sure as there's a heaven and as sure the stars do shine,
I'm gonna tease that dirty rascal when his troubles will be just like
   mine.

'Cause there ain't but one way you can keep a good woman down.
Lord, there ain't but one way to keep a good woman down.
You'll have to put her on an island and have her walk the bound.

"The Castle's Rockin'"

Come on by some night, my castle's rockin'.
You can bust your cunk cause everything's free.
On the top floor, in the rear is where I am residin', the stuff is here
   and the chicks fairly romp with glee.

You don't have to be afraid 'cause I'm payin' the boys to protect me.
Tell them cat's downtown they can let their conscience be.
Come on up, bring your gang, we'll start that ball a rollin',
My castle's rockin' run on by and see.

I say, come on up some night, my castle's rockin'.
You can bust your cunk cause everything's free.
On the top floor, in the rear, ah, that's where I am residin', the stuff
   is here and the chicks fairly romp with glee.

You don't have to be afraid 'cause I'm payin' the boys to protect me.
Tell them cat's downtown they can let their conscience be.
Ah, run on up, bring your gang, we'll start that ball a rollin',
Say, my castle's rockin', come on by and see.

"Boogie Woogie Swing"

There's a new kind a tune I'd like to sing to you,
It's a cross between the "Stomp" and the "Bally-Hoo"
It's full of rhythmical strain that really work on the brains,
And if you hear it once you want to hear it again.

A nice peppy tune with a ginger swing
It's got a groove kinda lilt that will make you sing.
It's mighty nice trumped with spice it's the "Boogie Woogie Classic
Swing."

Plunk that piano, Mr. Boogie man, please. Nice and slow so you can
render it with ease.
If you groove it on the after beat you'll see old and young shaggin'
down the street.

Play that "Boogie Woogie Swing" hey hey,
Every time you see me comin' down your way.
You can make me linger, make me walk that thing.
I'm talkin' 'bout that "Boogie Woogie Swing."

Plunk that piano, Mr. Boogie man, please. Nice and slow so you can
render it with ease.
If you groove it on the after beat you'll see old and young shaggin'
down the street.

Play that "Boogie Woogie Swing" hey hey,
Every time you see me comin' down your way.
You can make me linger, make me walk that thing.
I'm talkin' 'bout that "Boogie Woogie Swing."
I'm talkin' 'bout that "Boogie Woogie Swing."

"I Won't Let You Down"

So you say you're gonna leave me, that you're absolutely through.
If your mind is made up that way there is nothin' I can do.
Just remember these words, you'll want my love someday.
I gave you my affections, you shared everything I had. I double
crossed my poor own mother, even lied to my dear old dad.
I was just your slave, I loved and worshipped you.

When the hard luck overtake you and your glamour and charm are
gone,
When your high powered chicks forsake you and you just can't carry
on,
You can count on me, I won't let you down.

"Take Your Big Hands Off"

I got a pretty something a lot of cats would like to get.
But I won't let 'em have it cause it hasn't been used yet.
So take your big hands off it. Ooh, but wouldn't you like to have it?
They're plenty of others just like you.
You swear you're gonna get it; Well, you'll never live to tell it,
'Cause I'm savin' it for a man that's true.
Now I've made a vow to keep it and to that vow I'm holdin' on
And not a livin' Abe's gonna get it till the right man comes along.
So take your big hands off it.
I'll call the law if you try and touch it.
It's too good for a guy like you.
Yes, take your big claws off it.
I ain't thinkin' 'bout lettin' you touch it.
It's too delicate for a cat like you.
You're wastin' time to crave it.
I've made up my mind to save it for a man kind and true.
Now those flashin' eyes of yours may shine, and your pearly teeth
       may grit,
But not one peek of this precious thing of mine, brother, are you
       gonna get.
So take your big hands off it, I'll call the law if you try and touch it.

I'm talkin 'bout my big red rose.
It's too delicate for you.
I'm talkin' bout this big red rose.
Ain't that a shame?

"He's Got a Punch Like Joe Louis"

Lord, a woman is a fool to put all her trust in just one man.
Yes, a woman is a fool to put all her trust in just one man.
She can never get him when she wants him, just has to catch him
       when she can.

Yes, when I was crazy 'bout you, you were crazy 'bout somebody else.
Yes, when I was crazy 'bout you, you were crazy 'bout somebody else.

I know I was a fool to let you jive me, Lord, but I just couldn't help
    myself.

So get away from my window, stop knockin' on my door.
Lord, get away from my window, stop knockin' on my door.
'Cause I got myself some pig meat and I don't want you no more.
Spoken: Nice and young.

He's got a punch like Joe Louis and other charms that I admire.
He's got a punch like Joe Louis and other charms that I admire.
And when that baby starts in to love me, oh Lord, he starts my heart
    on fire.

Edith North Johnson

Edith North Johnson, also known as Maybelle Allen or Hattie North, was supposedly born in 1905 in St. Louis, Missouri (Harris). Before North made her debut as a singer, she worked as a saleslady in a music store owned by her husband, Jesse Johnson (Grattan).

While little biographical information may be found on Hattie North, much may be learned about her by reviewing the lyrics to her blues songs. One of her most popular songs, entitled "Honey Dripper Blues," touches the anxiety which apparently lies at the heart of women blues performers. This song discusses oppression within relationships, as the women during this time period were (or at least thought they were) at the mercy of their mistreating spouses. North depicts this dilemma in much the same manner as her contemporaries. In "Honey Dripper Blues" she says, "Oh, he treats me mean, only comes to see me sometimes. But the way he spreads his honey makes me think I'll lose my mind." While the spouse mentioned in this song is mean and cruel, North nevertheless expresses a love for her oppressor, which is common in many of the other blues songs pertaining to relationships.

"Honey Dripper Blues"

I wake up every morning with the rising sun.
I wake up every morning with the rising sun.
I'm thinking 'bout my honey dripper and all the wrongs he's done.

Oh, he treats me mean, only comes to see me sometimes.
Oh, he treats me mean, only comes to see me sometimes.
But the way he spreads his honey, makes me think I'll lose my mind.

Oh, 'cause I'm down, my good man wants to drive me away.
Oh, 'cause I'm down, Marty wants to drive me away.
But he's a good honey dripper, Lord, and I want him every day.

Now, the man I love, oh, Lord, he really made me fall.
Now, the man I love, oh, Lord, he really made me fall.
Oh, the way he drips his honey, you know he want my heart that's all.

Oh, sometimes I feel so lonesome, Lord, I don't know where to go.
Oh, sometimes I'm so lonesome, really don't know where to go.
And when my love comes down, I'll need you more than you'll ever
    know.

'Cause he's a real sweet man, gonna try and sign him up for ninety-
    nine.
Ah, he's a real sweet man, gonna try and sign him up for ninety-
    nine years.
That's what it takes to ease my mind and stop all of my tears.

——— Lil Johnson ———

Again, it is Dixon & Godrich who supply the only biographical information about female blues singer Lil Johnson. These two researchers inform us that Lil Johnson recorded "New Shave 'Em Dry" on November 19, 1936, on the Vocalian label in Chicago.

Judging from the song lyrics she performed, it is highly likely that Johnson toured the vaudeville circuit. All of her songs contain sexual innuendoes that imply vaudeville training, but perhaps "Press My Button (Ring My Bell)" contains the most blatant sexual references:

Come on baby, let's have some fun.
Just put your hot dog in my bun.
And I'll have that thing, that ding-a-ling.
Just press that button, give my bell a ring.

While most of her songs contain common sexual undertones, some contain implications that are less common, such as "You Stole My Cherry," in which she compares lovemaking to tree climbing:

Yes, I climbed and I climbed up the bark of a tree.
I climbed so high you stole my cherry from me.

Another such instance is in "Stavin' Chain" where she compares her body to a train, stating:

I'm the chief engineer, I'm gonna run it like Stavin' Chains.
Ah, grind baby, grind.

"My Baby (Squeeze Me Again)"

Squeeze me, squeeze me, squeeze me again.
Please don't stop till I tell you when.
Just squeeze me and love me some more.
Just like you did the other night before.

Now Misty Kissy is standin' close by.
Daddy, please don't make your sweet mama cry.
Just pick me up and set me on your knee.
'Cause I feel so good when you squeeze me.

Have you heard the story 'bout that little boy in the boat?
He don't wear no hat, he don't wear no overcoat,
He don't wear no stockings, don't wear no shoes,
But he's known to give a married man the weary blues.

He's slippery, and he's slimy, and just like grease,
He's got a breath that smells terrible just like your big feet.
Because I smelled it and I spied it and do you really know, that he's
    the most stinkin' little boy in the boat.

The funniest thing I ever saw in my life,
The dirty little boy stoled a married man's wife.
Now all you men you better work real fast,
'Cause that little boy is really shakin' the yas yas yas.

Don't come in fussin', don't raise no hell.
I can tell you been out by the way you smell.
I had a good man to give me everything,
But the last thing he give me he send me down to Hot Springs.

I'm long and lanky and built for speed.
I got everything that a good woman needs.
I ain't good lookin', ain't got no great curls.
But my mama gave me somethin' to carry me through this world.
I mean, carry me through this world.

"Honey You're So Good to Me"

What makes me treat you the way that I do?
Honey, you're so good to me.

I'd do anything for a man like you.
I'm wild about you, can't you see?
You got eyes like a tadpole, kiss like a frog,
and when you shimmy, baby, call that dog.
So, what makes me treat you the way that I do?
Honey, you're so good to me.
I mean, honey, you're so good to me.

Come on, baby, let's go to your room, I can't see that shakin'
        out here.
Come on, baby, let's go to your room, but (have my best friend Sher)
Let me have you long and hard,
Don't jive me with a little bit, I swear I want it all.
Come on, babe, let's go to your room, I can't stand that shakin' out
        here.
It gives me a thrill, I can't stand that shakin' out here.

Spoken: No, I can't stand that shakin' out here. I'm a cream puff.

What makes me suit you the way that I do?
Honey, you're so good to me.
I'd do anything for a man like you, I'm wild 'bout you, can't you see?
Now just because I'm low and squatty, don't mean that you don't
        want my hot body.
What makes me treat you the way that I do?
Honey, you're so good to me.
I mean, honey, you're so good to me.
What makes me treat you the way that I do?
Honey, you're so good to me.
I'd do anything for you, I'm wild 'bout you, can't you see?
Come on, baby, turn the lights down low.
When you say you're ready, come on, let's go.
What makes me treat you the way that I do?
Honey, you're so good to me.
I mean, honey, you're so good to me.

"New Shave 'Em Dry"

I want all you pimps and ramblers to gather round
While I dish you all the fresh low down.

I found a certain woman, I ain't gonna call her name,
But she round here oopy doopin' with her mama's man.
Now, Mother Harlem, now I'm gonna shave 'em dry.

She goes to bed every night and sleeps till twelve.
Get up and go, take those two (nails).
Now what she's doin' I can't understand.
All the neighbors say she's with her mama's man.
Now, Mother Harlem, now I'm gonna shave 'em dry.

Now she's the kind that don't kick 'em,
She'll take 'em in style,
If you're dumb enough to fall for her jive.
A dollar's a dollar and in God she trusts.
You're all right with her but those dollars come first.
Now, Mother Harlem, now I'm gonna shave 'em dry.

Now if you want something good and want it cheap,
You can go down on Eighteenth Street.
Step right in, get your money in your hand
You can get it anyway you want it then.
Now, Mother Harlem, now I'm gonna shave 'em dry.

I'm gonna tell you all women, and please understand,
Don't start no (please and nice) with my man.
'Cause if you do you'll surely get on wrong,
I got a .44 to put your waters on.
Now, Mother Harlem, now I'll shave you dry.

"Stavin' Chain"

If you don't shake, you won't get no cake.
If you don't hum, ain't gonna give you none.
You can't ride, honey, you can't ride this train.
I'm the chief engineer, and I'm gonna run it like Stavin' Chains.

I ask you in the mornin' to treat me right.
You put me off, tell me wait till night.
Now, you can't ride, honey, you can't ride this train.
I'm the chief engineer, I'm gonna run it like Stavin' Chains.

Take your horse outa my stable, back 'em out there.
I got another jockey, get yourself another man.
Now, you can't ride, honey, you can't ride this train.
I'm the chief engineer, I'm gonna run it like Stavin' Chains.

Stavin' Chain was a man of might.
He save up his money just to ride all night.
Now, you can't ride, honey, you can't ride this train.
I'm the chief engineer, I'm gonna run it like Stavin' Chains.
Ah, grind baby, grind.

I got to your house last night, 'bout half past four,
Found another woman comin' out your door.
Now, you can't ride, honey, you can't ride this train.
I'm the chief engineer, I'm gonna run it like Stavin' Chains.

"Press My Button (Ring My Bell)"

My man thought he was raisin' sin,
I said, "Give it to me, baby, you don't understand.
Would ya push that thing, would ya push that thing?
Just press that button, give my bell a ring.

Come on, baby, let's have some fun.
Just put your hot dog in my bun,
And I'll have that thing, that ding-a-ling.
Just press that button, give my bell a ring."

My man's out there in the raining cold.
He's got the right key but just can't find the hole.
He says, "Where's that thing, that ding-a-ling?
I been pressin' your button and your bell won't ring."
Spoken: Beat it out boys. Come on and oil my button.
　　　It's kinda rusty.

Now tell me, daddy, what it's all about.
Tryin' to fix your spark plug and it's all worn out.
I can't use that thing, that ding-a-ling.
I been pressin' your button and your bell won't ring.

You're my baby, all outa breath,
Been workin' all night and ain't done nothin' yet.

Said, what's wrong with that thing, that ding-a-ling?
I been pressin' your button and your bell won't ring.

Hear me, baby, on my bending knees.
I want some kind daddy, just to hear my plea.
And bring me that thing, that ding-a-ling.
Just press my button, give my bell a ring.

"You Stole My Cherry"

How do you want me to love you, when you keep on holdin' yours
   back?
Why you must think your mama has got rubber in her back.
Now you start in to kissin', I ask you to stop.
But I could not be good 'cause those kisses were hot.
When it comes to lovin', you all right with me,
'Cause you got everything that a good man needs.

Yes I twirl and I twirl, baby, I twirl from right to left.
And if you want anymore lovin', baby, you'll have to twirl yourself.
Yes I climbed and I climbed like a fox up a tree.
I climbed so high you stole my cherry from me.
How do you want me to love you, when you keep on holdin' yours
   back?

How do you want me to love you, when baby, you keep on holdin'
   yours back?
Why you must think your mama has got rubber in her back.
Now you start in to kissin', I ask you to stop.
But I could not be good 'cause those kisses were hot.
When it comes to lovin', you all right with me,
'Cause you got everything that a good man needs.

I twirl and I twirl, baby, I twirl from right to left.
And if you want anymore lovin', you'll have to twirl yourself.
When my gate goes up and my love comes down,
I gets on your trail like a thirsty bloodhound.
How do you want me to love you, when baby, you keep on holdin'
   yours back?
I mean, oh babe, you keep on, keep on holdin' yours back.

"Keep Your Hands Off It"

Don't come in here fussin', don't raise no spam.
You didn't want it when you had it, so I got another man.
Keep your hands off it.
Oh, keep your hands off it.
Just keep your hands off it, 'cause it don't belong to you.

I've got nuts in my bag, nice and brown.
Got a sweet man to bust 'em when he comes around.
So keep your hands off it.
Oh, keep your hands off it.
Just keep your hands off it, 'cause it don't belong to you.

You like to churn my mill, just when you hear me scream,
You turn the mill thicker and rich like cream.
So keep your hands off it.
Oh, keep your hands off it.
Just keep your hands off it, 'cause it don't belong to you.

He calls me his cookie 'cause I'm so sweet.
He says I got something that can't be beat.
So keep your hands off it.
Oh, keep your hands off it.
Just keep your hands off it, 'cause it don't belong to you.

——Mary Johnson——

Mary Johnson was born in 1900 in Eden Station, Mississippi (Harris). She married another blues singer, Lonnie Johnson, and bore six of his children in their seven years of marriage (Harris). According to Grattan, Mary Johnson spent most of her life in St. Louis. Her singing career began when she won a blues contest; the prize was a record contract with Paramount. Although Johnson sang in many different clubs and bars, she maintained her steady income by working in a hospital (Grattan).

Perhaps her relationship with Lonnie led her to believe in the lyrics to the song "Muddy Creek Blues," which states, "I'd rather be in a muddy creek, Lord, than to lack my love," as it is obvious that her career in music as well as her nursing career would have been much more difficult without a husband to help her with her children.

"Muddy Creek Blues"

I'd rather be in a muddy creek, Lord, than to lack my love.
I'd rather be in a muddy creek, Lord, than to lack my love.
Than to be insane, Lord, really (treated like a poor white dove).

I went to the muddy creek this mornin' with my razor swingin' in
my hand.
I went to the muddy creek this mornin' with my razor swingin' in
my hand.
I said, "Good mornin' Mr. Tadpole, have you seen anything of my
man?"

The tadpole bowed to me before I raised my head.
The tadpole bowed to me before I raised my head.
"I'm tellin' you, dear lady, I'm not keepin' up with your man."

I say I'm black and evil, you sure don't know my mind.
I say I'm black and evil, you sure don't know my mind.
I try talkin' 'bout Mr. Tadpole, drink your blood like cherry wine.

"Room Rent Blues"

My room rent is due this mornin', I did not have a dime.
My room rent is due this mornin', I did not have a dime.
The landlord told me he'd give me till half past nine.

I said, "Kind papa, will you please give me a chance?"
Oh, please give me a chance.
I'll get myself some money, and pay my room rent in advance.

I'm just a poor girl, I don't have no place to go.
I'm just a poor girl, have no place to go.
I haven't got no good man, and I'm driftin' from door to door.

I'm goin' to the radio station with my boss on the air.
I'm goin' to the radio station with my boss on the air.
And maybe by broadcastin', I can pay my room rent somewhere.

—— Virginia Liston ——

Virginia Liston was born in 1890, and died in June of 1932, in St. Louis, Missouri (Harris). By the time Liston was 22, she was singing the blues, and by 1920 she was living in New York and performing in Harlem theaters (Grattan).

Liston toured the TOBA vaudeville circuit, and her song "I've Got What It Takes," has all the characteristics of vaudeville. In this song, Liston seems to be referring to her virginity when she says, "I've been saving it up for a mighty long time. To give it away would be more than a crime." However, she is actually referring to money, which is obvious when she says, "Now you want my money and it's my plan to save it all for a real good man."

"I've Got What It Takes"

I've got what it takes but it breaks my heart to give it away.
It's in demand and it's something wanted every day.
I've been savin' it up for a mighty long time.
To give it away would be more than a crime.
(He rides me wrong, he cheats me quick), but none of my small
    change shall you get.
I'll let you look at my bankbook but I'll never let you feel my purse.
Daddy, take your hands away, I believe in safety first.
Now you want my money, and it's my plan to save it all for a real
    good man.
I've got what it takes but it breaks my heart to give it away.

Lil Mae

Information about the next singer, Lil Mae, is not available; however, the lyrics to the song she performed called "Wise Like That" suggest that what she learned in life she learned the hard way:

Now, I went drillin' down the avenue with a married man.
I saw a woman comin' with a pistol in her hand.
And I got wise like that, wise like that I mean.
And every day has brought me somethin' I ain't never seen.

The refrain to this song "And every day has brought me somethin' I ain't never seen," implies the common belief that knowledge may be obtained only from what is experienced, and Mae admits this when she says:

Now, I ain't no carpenter, but I know the rules.
I ain't no clapper, but I could really use your shoes.
I'm just wise like that, wise like that I mean.
And every day has brought me somethin' I ain't never seen.

Mae's song is important to the blues collection because it asserts that textbook learning will not always be the most beneficial, and like other blues songs, it subscribes to the belief that the only way someone may truly know something is by doing it or seeing it.

"Wise Like That"

Now you can go the country and get yourself a man.
But you can't tell him how to love you, he already understands.

He's just wise like that, wise like that I mean.
And every day has brought me somethin' I ain't never seen.

Now from the cradle to the crutches it's ninety percent true,
If you don't give them what they ask for men'll take it all from you.
They're just wise like that, wise like that I mean.
And every day has brought me somethin' I ain't never seen.

Now, I ain't no carpenter, but I know the rules.
I ain't no clapper, but I could really use your shoes.
I'm just wise like that, wise like that I mean.
And every day has brought me somethin' I ain't never seen.

Now the monkey told the baboon, that baby sure's mean.
Beats me about an ape that you ain't never seen.
He's just wise like that, wise like that I mean.
And every day has brought me somethin' I ain't never seen.

I got me two or three bottles of barley, three or four quarts of rye.
Chuck my head out in the alley and kick my heels high.
'Cause I'm just wise like that, wise like that I mean.
And every day has brought me somethin' I ain't never seen.

Now, I went drillin' down the avenue with a married man.
I saw a woman comin' with a pistol in her hand.
And I got wise like that, wise like that I mean.
And everyday has brought me somethin' I ain't never seen.

———— Alice Moore ————

Alice Moore's life story does not appear in any blues encyclopedia. What we do know about Moore is that she recorded the song "Lonesome Dream Blues" in November of 1929, in Grafton, Wisconsin (Dixon & Godrich). "Lonesome Dream Blues" appears as a perpetual lament for the man that left her. The song exists in the twelve bar blues form. While she begins to tell her story by referring to it as a dream, at the end of the song we know that her man has really left her. Her state of despair may be heard in the words as well as the rhythm of this song.

Another song performed by Moore called "Kidman Blues" sticks to the same style and theme:

> Baby, when I was all down and out, you just could not be found.
> Baby, when I was all down and out, you just could not be found.
> Now I've got someone to care for me, don't want you hangin' around.

Heartache and bad relationships seem to be a specialty for Moore, as the end of "Kidman Blues" woefully states:

> Just a poor little gal lookin' in the deep blue sea.
> Just a poor little girl lookin' in the deep blue sea.
> I done quit you, kidman, so don't sing your blues to me.

"Lonesome Dream Blues"

Had a dream last night, babe, I can't understand.
Had a dream last night, babe, I can't understand.
I dreamed I saw some woman teasin' with my man.

89

I tried to be good, but he wouldn't let me in.
I tried to be good, but he would not let me in.
Now he is leavin', just to spite poor me.

Now, you got all my money still you ain't satisfied.
Now, you got all my money still you ain't satisfied.
And now you got another woman that you can sit dreamin' by.

You made your choice, you may have your way.
You made your choice, you may have your way.
I mean you take all your lovin', I know that you cannot stay.

—— Monette Moore ——

Monette Moore, alias Ethel Myers, Nettie Potter, Susie Smith or Grace White, was born on May 19, 1902, in Gainesville, Texas, and died on October 21, 1962, in Garden Grove, California (Harris). Her death was due to an attack of emphysema (Harris). Throughout the whole of her life, Moore sang for record labels, in clubs and theaters and, in fact, she was in the middle of a gig at Disneyland when the emphysema attack occurred (Harris).

Moore knew a great deal about the troubles that make the blues, and her songs contain complaints such as lack of money in "House Rent Blues," inadequate working conditions in "Workhouse Blues," and the desperation which leads a woman to leave her man in "The Bye Bye Blues":

> Now I feel blue, I'm going to do something that may look wrong.
> When my man comes he'll be surprised to find that I am gone.
> I've just found out we can't agree, no matter how I try.
> I wrote a note, will get his throat, when he reads this last goodbye;

Moore also sang about the problems of racism in "Black Sheep Blues":

> Lord, from the straight and narrow path I've strayed.
> From the straight and narrow path I've strayed.
> With regret and sorrows I have paid.
> Just a black sheep roamin' round the town.
> Just a black sheep roamin' round the town.
> Like a tramp, I'm always out and down;

and reaction to death in "Undertaker Blues":

Cemetery sure is one lonesome place.
Cemetery sure is a lonesome place.
When you're dead they throw dirt in your face.

Moore sang the blues on a number of topics, and each of her blues songs sends a message of misery to the listener.

"House Rent Blues"

Spoken: Lord, I'm broke. And here come that rent man again.

On a cold, dark and stormy night,
On a cold, dark and stormy night,
They wanted to put me out and it wasn't daylight.

There on my door they nailed a sign.
There on my door they nailed a sign.
I got to leave from here if the rent man don't change his mind.

When you see me comin', put your woman outdoors.
When you see me comin', put your woman outdoors.
You know I ain't no stranger, cause' I been here before.

Oh, Lawdy what a feelin', rent man comes a creepin', in my bed asleepin'. He left me with those house rent blues.

"Workhouse Blues"

Everybody's tryin' the workhouse through the day, oh, Lord.
Oh, Lord, the work is so hard, thirty days is so long, oh, Lord.
Oh, Lord, I can't cry, I can't cook, if I run away, will that be good?
'Cause I'm goin to the (Maze I'm goin' to the capital).

Yes, Lord, I'm bound for the (Maze I'm goin' to the capital).
I've got to leave here, got to catch the next train gone.

Workhouse sets way up on a long ole lonesome road.
Workhouse sets way up on a lonesome road.
I'm a hard luck gal, catch the devil everywhere I go.

Say, I wish I had a heaven of my own.
Lord, I wish I had a heaven of my own.
I'd give this whole world for some happy home.

He used to be mine, but look who's got him now.
He used to be mine, look who's got him now.
You sure can keep him, he don't mean no good no how.

Hazel Myers

Biographical information on Hazel Myers is unobtainable, but her style and tone comply with those of other women performers who toured vaudeville. "You'll Never Have No Luck by Quittin' Me" supplies practical advice for her boyfriend, who leaves her as she warns him that what goes around comes around:

> You'll never have no luck by quittin' me, someone will treat you the
> same way, you see.

This was a common theme for the vaudeville performers.

Two other songs recorded by Hazel Myers also stick to prevalent themes of vaudeville. "Lonesome For That Man of Mine" discusses the misery she feels when her lover is away:

> He went away and left me flat and I'm worried 'bout him all the
> time.
> Now, I don't know why he did leave but I know he sure did cause my
> heart to bleed.
> That's why I'm lonesome, lonesome, lonesome for that man of mine.

Myers laments that she has no control over the fact that her man has left her, which partially explains her need for drugs in "Pipe Dream Blues:"

> I burned up ten thousand dollar bills.
> I burned up ten thousand dollar bills.
> Guess I burn them every time I'd like my fill.

Here we see how living conditions could lead a woman to be so dependent on drugs that she dreams about marijuana and doesn't worry about how much money she needs to spend on it.

"You'll Never Have No Luck By Quittin' Me"

We've been together, daddy, all of these years,
Now you are drivin' me to trouble and tears.
Today, today you're leaving and you know you'll leave me grieving.
You may have another mama to take my place,
One you can meet with a smiling face.
But if you're goin' away, dear, for to stay, I want you to remember
    what I say.
You'll never have no luck by quittin' me, someone will treat you the
    same way, you see.
No one knows what I've gone through.
Catch me fighting everything, dear, just for you.
Yes, you may have your chitlin's all arranged,
But you'll find out that things can change.
For sooner or later you are bound to see,
You'll never have no luck by quittin' me.
You'll never have no luck by quittin' me.
You'll never have no luck by quittin' me, you're gonna see dark days
    and misery.
No good luck will come to you.
You'll fail in everything you try to do.
Someday you'll love someone, as I do you,
Then you'll know what I've gone through.
For sooner or later you are bound to see,
You'll never have no luck by quittin' me.
You'll never have no luck by quittin' me.

——— Jenny Pope ———

Jenny Pope, alias Jennie Clayton, often sang with the Memphis Jug Band (Dixon & Godrich). "Bull Frog Blues" was recorded in February, 1930, on the Vocalian label in Memphis (Dixon & Godrich). Pope wrote and performed many blues songs, including the two that follow.

"Tennessee Workhouse Blues"

Said Bill's in the workhouse way out in muddy Tennessee.
Said Bill's in the workhouse way out in muddy Tennessee.
That's where they take the prisoners, they never set them free.

They take my daddy to the workhouse, they put him down on
    the rock.
They take my daddy to the workhouse, they put him down on
    the rock.
Just because he lives with prisoners they had him a secret dock.

He was charged with murder, but stealin' was his crime.
He was charged with murder, but stealin' was his crime.
He stole my daddy and had to serve his time.

I went to a lawyer, I call him over the phone.
I went to a lawyer, I call him over the phone.
Said, listen, Mr. Lawyer, when will my man be home?

That workhouse, workhouse is way out on a lonesome road.
That workhouse, workhouse is way out on a lonesome road.
I hate to see my daddy carry that heavy load.

96

"Bullfrog Blues"

Hey ey ey, oh, oh, oh, bullfrog blues is really on my mind.
They're all in my bedroom, drinkin' up my wine.

Hey, pretty papa, hey, pretty papa, I can't stand these bullfrog blues
    no more.
They're all in my cabinets, hoppin' all over my floor.

I woke up this mornin' to make a fire on the stove.
I woke up this mornin' to make a fire on the stove.
Bullfrog's in the breadcase chasin' after those jelly rolls.

Hey, Mr. Bullfrog, hey, I'm gonna tell you all, I can't stand your
    girly girl in here.
You can go out in the backyard, I'll leave the pallets there.

I will make you a pallet so you can jelly roll.
I will make you a pallet so you can jelly roll.
And you can cook me breakfast right on my brand new floor.

——— Ma Rainey ———

Gertrude Rainey, otherwise and most often known as Ma or Madame Rainey, was born April 26, 1886, in Columbus, Georgia, and died on December 22, 1939, in Columbus, Georgia (Harris). Ma Rainey is one of the most well known female blues artist from her time period and biographical information concerning her life is easily obtainable.

Along with the abundance of biographical information pertaining to Ma Rainey, many rumors about her life have also circulated. One such rumor is that Ma Rainey and her husband Pa Rainey kidnapped Bessie Smith, another prominent female blues singer, and forced her to travel with them in their traveling tent show. It is also said that during this time Ma Rainey taught Bessie Smith how to sing. While Ma Rainey did perform in a traveling tent show, it is more accurate to say that she and Bessie Smith were good friends.

Ma Rainey's style is very much related to folk music in that she sings about issues much like the men do in the downhome or urban blues. Some of the topics of her blues songs include breaking the law and going to jail as in "Chain Gang Blues," superstition as in "Wringing and Twisting the Blues," intoxication as a relief from having the blues as in "Dead Drunk Blues," and the problems of relationships as in the song "Daddy, Goodbye Blues."

"Dead Drunk Blues"

Oh, gimme Houston, that's the place I crave.
Oh, gimme Houston, that's the place I crave.
Oh, way down south I'll take whiskey (straight).

Oh, whiskey, whiskey, in from old down home.
Oh, whiskey, whiskey, in from old down home.
But if I don't get whiskey I ain't no good at all.

When I was in Houston drunk most everyday.
When I was in Houston drunk most everyday.
I drank so much whiskey I thought I'd pass away.

Have you ever been drunk, slept in all of your clothes?
Have you ever been drunk, slept in all of your clothes?
And when you wake up you'll find you're out of doors.

Daddy, I'm gonna get drunk, just one more time.
Honey, I'm gonna get drunk, papa, just one more time.
'Cause when I'm drunk nothin' gonna worry my mind.

"New Bo-Weevil Blues"

Hey, bo-weevil, don't sing them blues no more.
Hey, hey, bo-weevil, don't sing them blues no more.
Bo-Weevils here, bo-weevils everywhere you go.

I'm a lone bo-weevil been out a great long time.
I'm a lone bo-weevil been out a great long time.
I'm gonna sing these blues for these the bo-weevil lonesome lines.

I don't want no man to put no sugar in my tea.
I don't want no man to put no sugar in my tea.
Some of 'em so evil I'm afraid they might poison me.

Lord, I went downtown and bought me a hat,
I brought it back home and laid it on the shelf.
Looked at my bed, I'm gettin' tired sleepin' by myself.

"Moonshine Blues"

I been drinkin' all night, babe, and the night before.
When I get sober, ain't gonna drink no more.
'Cause my (feet, head and hands are in the door).

My head goes round and I around
since my daddy left town.

(I don't know the river down in the Harlem town).
But there's one thing certain, mama gonna be leavin' town.
You'll find me regal and a rockin',
Howlin' like a hound.
Catch the first train that's goin' South bound.
No, stop, you hear me say stop.
Like a my brain, oh, stop that train.
So I can ride back home again.
Here I'm upon my knees.
Put out again (I see)
For I'm about to be
Settin' my mind at ease
'Cause I can't stand 'em
Can't stand 'em
The man I love, the man from town
I felt like screamin', I feel like cryin', Lord,
I been defeated so's I don't mind dyin'
I'm bound home, I'm gonna settle down.
I'm bound South now, gotta slow down.
Tell everybody I'm on my way, Lord.
I got the moonshine blues, I say,
I got the moonshine blues.

"Blame It on the Blues"

I'm so sad and worried, got no time to spread the news.
I'm so sad and worried, got no time to spread the news.
Won't blame it on my troubles, can't blame it on the blues.

Lawd, Lawd, Lawdy, Lawdy, Lawd.
Lawd, Lawd, Lawdy, Lawdy, Lawd.
Lawd, Lawd, a Lawd, Lawd, Lawd.
Lawd, who'm I gonna blame it on then?

I can't blame my daddy, he's been nice and kind.
I can't blame my daddy, he's been nice and kind.
Well, I blame it on my mistakes, blame it on that trouble of mine.

This house is like a graveyard when I live here by myself.
This house is like graveyard when I live here by myself.
Well, I blame it on my lover, blame it on somebody else.

Can't blame my mother, can't blame my dad, can't blame my brother
     for the trouble I've had.
Can't blame my lover that held my hand, can't blame my husband,
     can't blame my man.
Can't blame nobody, guess I'll have to blame it on the blues.

"Hustlin' Blues"

It's rainin' out here, and tricks ain't walkin' tonight.
It's rainin' out here, and tricks ain't walkin' tonight.
I'm goin' home, I know I got to fight.

If you hit me tonight, let me tell you what I'm goin' to do.
If you hit me tonight, let me tell you what I'm goin' to do.
I'm goin' to take you to court and tell the judge on you.

I ain't made no money and he dared me to go home.
I ain't made no money and he dared me to go home.
(you're a dark fool baby) and you better leave me alone.

He followed me up and he grabbed me for a fight.
He followed me up and he grabbed me for a fight.
He said, "Lord, don't you know you ain't made no money tonight?"

Oh, go tell him I'm through.
Oh, go tell him I'm through.
I'm tired of this life, that's why I brought it to you.

"Log Camp Blues"

Down in Mississippi, (where I am goin' down).
Down in Mississippi, (where I am goin' down).
Go down on the Delta, is a great big loggin' camp.

I can see my daddy, jumpin' around from log to log.
I can see my daddy, jumpin' around from log to log.
('Cause down in ole Chicago everybody's on the hog.)

Throw away your paint, daddy, (burn up your pants to wear.)
Throw away your paint, daddy, (burn up your pants to wear.)
Get your overhauls and jumpers, start the rollin' car down there.

Melons in my meat box, chicken runs around my yard.
Melons in my meat box, chicken runs around my yard.
Young'uns in my coffin, I never knew the time was hard.

If I can't get no ticket, put on my walkin' shoes.
If I can't get no ticket, put on my walkin' shoes.
I'm goin to Mississippi, singin' the "Loggin' Camp Blues."

—— Issie Ringgold ——

Although Issie Ringgold almost always went by the name Issie, her birth name was Muriel (Dixon & Godrich). The two songs "He's a Good Meat Cutter" and "Be on Your Merry Way," appearing on the next pages, were both recorded on Wednesday, January 22, 1930, on the Columbia Label in New York City (Dixon & Godrich).

Both songs make derogatory remarks about men. The refrain to "He's a Good Meat Cutter" is evidence enough for her lack of trust in men:

> He's a good meat cutter, keeps his mind in the gutter,
> But he don't mean you no good.

And "Be on Your Merry Way" further exhibits this notion explicitly:

> You said you loved me, do you know any more funny jokes?
> Ah, you're gonna be sweet when you done lost your daily strokes.
> You stay out every night until half past three.
> And when you get home you turn your back on me.
> Looks like if I want to see you I got to send you a telegram.
> What kind of a woman do you think I am?

Ringgold's lack of trust for the man she dates generalizes into a commonly held belief that all men are compelled to be infidels.

"He's a Good Meat Cutter"

There's a butcher on the corner they call Bopeep.
And his butcherin' can't be beat.

He's a good meat cutter, keeps his mind in the gutter,
But he don't mean you no good.

He did some cuttin' for Della, and sent some back.
Brother Peter hollered out, "What kind of a butcher is that?"
He's a good meat cutter, keeps his mind in the gutter,
But he don't mean you no good.

Now it's not like he's cuttin', he always smiles.
He cuts a little bit, then rest awhile.
He's a good meat cutter, keeps his mind in the gutter,
But he don't mean you no good.

His cuttin' hours are from twelve to five.
He'll cut a little longer if you ain't satisfied.
He's a good meat cutter, keeps his mind in the gutter,
But he don't mean you no good.

If you want some meat, fresh and fine,
Call around his market, 'bout half past nine.
He's a good meat cutter, keeps his mind in the gutter,
But he don't mean you no good.

You'll like his meat, don't care how much it costs.
If you don't get full weight, you ain't nothing lost.
He's a good meat cutter, keeps his mind in the gutter,
But he don't mean you no good.

When he starts to cuttin' he's a cuttin' cat.
All the girls they say he's really tight like that.
He's a good meat cutter, keeps his mind in the gutter,
But he don't mean you no good.

Just as sure as that blind hog found that acorn tree.
That meat cuttin' man is goin' to be the death of me.
He's a good meat cutter, keeps his mind in the gutter,
But he don't mean you no good.

"Be on Your Merry Way"

Listen here, Bill Jackson.
I'm really tired of you.

You may look good to someone else, but I don't like the way you do.
So, pack your truck and leave. Ain't no use in you gettin' peeved.
Say you may be all right, but honey, you really ain't my type.
You'll never stick your foot under my table no more.
Don't you know what I mean when I say go?
Well, you'll not put on them pajamas, but that can wait,
But you ain't gonna park in my brown skinned bed.
You'll miss your eggs, hot ham, and toast, chicken dumplings and
     my good pot roast.
That good cold, nigger, what made you see double.
You'll miss my sewing so. What gave you so much trouble? I mean
     trouble.
So your pleadin' and your cryin' won't do you no good.
'Cause you done got too old to do the things you should.
So cold papa, be on your merry way.

You said you loved me, do you know any more funny jokes?
Ah, you're gonna be sweet when you done lost your daily strokes.
You stay out every night until half past three.
And when you get home you turn your back on me.
Looks like if I want to see you I got to send you a telegram.
What kind of a woman do you think I am?
Why here you are fifty-nine and I'm sixteen full of spice.
If you want me to love you, honey, you got to treat me nice.
So let me miss you, papa, cause we can't agree.
And if you never come back, it will be soon enough for me.
I don't even want to see you on a judgment day.
So, cold papa, be on your merry way.
I mean be on your merry way.

───── Irene Scruggs ─────

Irene Scruggs, also called Chocolate Brown, Little Sister and Dixie Nolan, was on December 7, 1901, in Mississippi; the date of her death is not reported (Harris). Irene Scruggs traveled and worked on the TOBA circuit and also worked in several clubs, playing with prominent male blues performers such as Lonnie Johnson and Little Brother Montgomery (Harris).

Even though Scruggs performed in some of the rougher juke joints, her style greatly conforms to that of vaudeville, as evidenced in her song "Must Get Mine in Front," which implicitly refers to sexual activity in the form of prostitution. In this song, Scruggs refers to "Susie," who runs a bakery shop and does not allow people to take from her bakery on credit. However, in the remainder of the song, it becomes obvious that Scruggs is not only referring to business transactions at the bakery shop. When Scruggs says, "No, I ain't puttin' out nothin' till you pay off," "puttin' out" takes on the connotation of the phrase that means giving away sexual favors. The parallel between business transactions at the bakery shop and business transactions in prostitution relays a hidden meaning and makes it possible for Scruggs to talk about prostitution without using any offensive language.

"Must Get Mine in Front"

Susie runs a bakery shop down the street,
Sells jelly cakes that always look neat.
Sam hung around, said, mama, give me a break, I want you to credit
    me for some of that cake.

I'm goin up the river, got a job loadin' sacks,
pay you for that cake when I get back.

She looked at him and said, Don't be no ham.
What kind of fool do you think I am? Some folks may trust you,
    some, I can't say. I must get mine in front. I'll trust you
    tomorrow if you pay me today. I must get mine in front.
Now you go on up the river and you carry your sacks. This jelly roll
    will be here when you get back.
I trusted the man who lived next door and since then he don't speak
    to me no more.
I trusted a man who said he be back again.
The very next day he took a trip to Spain.
I trusted your father, he ain't no good.
He owes every woman in the neighborhood.
Some folks may trust you to come back and pay, I must get mine in
    front.
Hear me talkin', I must get mine in front.

Now your uncle owes me he sure has bad taste.
He must think I got this stuff to give away.
No, I ain't puttin' out nothin', 'til you pay off.
I must get mine in front. I ain't jokin', I must get mine in front.

—— Bessie Smith ——

Bessie Smith was born on April 15, 1894, in Chattanooga, Tennessee, and died on September 26, 1937, in Clarksdale, Mississippi (Harris). Like Ma Rainey, Bessie Smith is a well-known blues artist of this seminal era. Smith toured on the TOBA circuit of vaudeville, and much of the music performed at the onset of her career conforms to the vaudeville style. Her first big hit, "Downhearted Blues," discusses the issue of a mistreating man, a common theme for women blues performers. In this song, she uses language that is appropriate and acceptable for the vaudeville circuit.

However, rumor states that Bessie Smith was often quite defiant and hard to work with. She frequently engaged in homosexual affairs (supposedly with Ma Rainey), drank moonshine and used foul language whenever possible. So, it is not surprising that the music that she performed later on in her career was untypical of the style that was expected of her. Songs like "Gimme a Pigfoot" express her inability to conform in no uncertain terms. The beginning of the song states, "Twenty-five cents, oh no, I wouldn't pay twenty-five cents to go in nowhere!" Although Smith knew what was expected of her, she had her own agenda to tend to.

"Do Your Duty"

You come home three times a day, baby, come and drive my blues
    away.
When you come, be ready to play.
Do your duty.

If you want to have some love, give your baby your last buck.
Don't come quackin' like a duck.
Do your duty.

I heard you say you didn't love me, baby,
You sit here and admit Mrs. Brown.
I don't believe a word she said.
She's the lyingest woman in town.
Oh babe, when I need to take a man home,
I'll just call you on the telephone.
Come yourself, don't bring your friend Joan,
Do your duty.

If my raving gets too hot,
Cool it off, here, that's the spot.
Gimme all the service you got.
Do your duty, baby.

If you don't know what it's all about,
Don't sit around my house and pout.
Till you catch your mama tippin' out,
Do your duty.

If you make your own bed hard,
That's the way of life.
If I'm tired of sleepin' by myself,
you're too dumb to realize.
Oh babe, I'm not tryin' to make you feel blue.
I'm not satisfied with the way that you do.
I've got to help you find somebody to
Do your duty.

"Faraway Blues" (with Clara Smith)

We laughed by the southern home.
I wander the lonesome road.
Blackbirds went seeking a brand new field of corn.

We don't know why we are here.
But we are all here just the same.
And we are just a long time here, just to save our boys.

Some of these days, we are going far away.
Some of these days, we are going far away.
When we are far, a lot of friends
(And don't have no room to bring you back).

There'll come a day when from us you'll have no news.
So, there'll come a day when from us you'll have no news.
Then you will know that we have died from the lonesome far away
    blues.

Clara Smith

Clara Smith, known also as Violet Green, was born in 1894 in Spartanburg, South Carolina, and died on February 2, 1935, in Detroit, Michigan (Harris). Clara Smith (no relation to Bessie Smith) left home while she was still very young to tour on the vaudeville circuit (Harris). Smith began singing in theaters as early as 1910, and during the 1930s she sang at the Stroller's Club in New York City and Orchestra Gardens in Detroit (Claghorn).

Many of her songs, such as "I Ain't Got Nobody to Grind My Coffee," and "Daddy, Don't Put That Thing on Me," mark the continuous struggle in male-female relationships. The songs portray the woman's need for a man to support her and the woman's complete helplessness without a man. Smith's song "It's Tight Like That" is another classic example of a vaudeville song. At the beginning of the song she says, "Listen here, folks, I'm gonna sing a little song. But you mustn't get mad, I don't mean no wrong." Here, Smith is asking to be excused for any language that may be considered crass.

"Race Track Blues"

Look where the evening's come so far.
That night done come and I'm all alone.
My easy rider left this town;
He said he was New Orleans bound.
I'm writing him a letter today.
And this is what I'm goin' to say:
Easy rider, what are you doing today?

111

Ain't got no horse, ain't got no jockey,
Ain't had a winner since you went away.
You were rough and tough, oh, to me.
But you sure could ride them ponies for me.
Ain't bettin' no money, ain't goin' to the tracks.
Gonna keep my barn empty till you get back.
Ain't gonna buy no wool, ain't gonna sell no corn.
Won't water no mules in my trough while you are gone.
Easy rider, I am all alone.
My easy rider, won't you please come home?

Easy rider, I feel all alone.
My easy rider, won't you please come home?

"Wanna Go Home"

I've got a home, (he bugged me gone).
I've got a home, (he bugged me gone).
I've got a home, like to tell you, friend of mine.
I heard my daddy when he knocked on my door.
Shoes and stockings in his hand, feet on the floor.
I bet he's got your heart and he take your hand.
Come with me, you won't go back there no more.

Mmmmmm, Mmmmmmmm, Mmmmmmmmmm,
    Mmmmmmmmmm.
Mmmmmm, Mmmmmmmm, Mmmmmmmmmm,
    Mmmmmmmmmm.
Wanna go home. Wanna go home, daddy. Don't you want to go?

"I Ain't Got Nobody to Grind My Coffee"

Once I had a lovin' daddy, just as sweet as he could be.
But my ever lovin' daddy, he's done gone from me.
And since he's left me behind, guess what's on my mind?
I ain't got nobody to grind my coffee in the morning.
Ain't got nobody to serve my breakfast in bed.

My daddy went away, leaves me alone today.
How am I gonna find another puppy blinder,
Who would do my grindin' like my sweet daddy would?

I ain't got nobody to light my brand new percolator.
Ain't got nobody to heat my oven to heat.
When my daddy used to love me he was, oh, so good.
He would take out all my ashes, even chop my kindling wood.
Ain't got nobody who could love me like he could and do my
    grindin' for me.

My daddy used to love me (three hours a day).
Believe me he could do it different from the rest.
Ain't got nobody who could put me to a test,
And do my grindin' for me, I said,
And do my grindin' for me.

"Daddy Don't Put That Thing on Me"

I'm goin' down to the track to see that snake charmin' man.
The man that's got that big black thing wrapped around his head.
Right down in Dallas, I'll deliver this plea.
Mr. snake charmin' papa, have mercy on me.
That's what I say before the undertaker take me away.
Oh, daddy, don't you put that thing on me.
I don't like it very much.
Daddy, don't you put that thing on me.
I simply can't stand the touch.
Don't like the way it looks, especially tanned.
If you put it on me, papa, you will kill me dead.
You hear me screaming you know what I'm meaning.
Don't you put that thing on me.

I know a big handsome papa, called the snake charming king.
A man that loves to chauffeur that big black thing.
He's just as right as any man can be.
But he loves to put that thing on children like me.
Guess what I'll say if I just see him start comin' my way?
Oh, don't you dare to put that thing on me.

Go ahead, and let me be.
Now you know that very well I can't stand that thing put on me,
    gives me such a chill.
I don't like the way it looks, especially twists,
If you put that thing on my hand put it around my wrist.
You hear me screaming, you know what I'm meaning.
Don't you dare to put that thing on me.

"My John Blues"

Wake up man, when you're bright the sun does shine.
Wake up man, when you're bright the sun does shine.
Get up with that sunshine gang and bring me here sometime.

Now he ain't got no teeth and (beams as low as you toes).
He ain't got no teeth and (beams as low as you toes).
Now, you know, man, you got to bring me here some dough.

Now the meal in the barrel is going bad.
How long, man, do you think the (powder logs) last?
Rip Van Winkle slept for a long long time,
But Rip Van Winkle was no man of mine.

I don't want a man that don't work every day.
I want a man that brings home his pay.
So get out of that bed, man, be on your way.
You ramble all night and you sleep all day.
So now, I'm cross, and now I'm feelin' bad.
So now I'm cross and I'm feelin' mad.
'Cause you're the laziest man that I ever had.

"Courthouse Blues"

I gave my daddy a bottle of beer and a glass of ale, Lord.
I give him beer, then a glass of ale.
Told him this time tomorrow I'll be layin' in that crowded jail.
I mean the crowded jail.

Three months in jail ain't no long, long, long time.
Three months in jail ain't no long, long time.
The man I love, he made ninety-nine.

The jury men been on my case from eight till three.
Jury men sit on my case from eight till three.
And the verdict was, let the poor gal go free.
I mean the gal go free.

I sit in the courthouse with my face in my hands.
I sit in the courthouse face hid in my hands.
And it's all on account of one triflin' man.
I mean one triflin' man.

"Kitchen Mechanic Blues"

Women talk about me and lie about me, cuss me out of my name.
They talk about me and lie about me, cuss me out of my name.
All their men come to see me just the same.

I'm just a workin' gal, poor workin' gal, kitchen mechanic is what
    they say.
I'm just a workin' gal, poor workin' gal, kitchen mechanic is what
    they say.
But I'll have an honest dollar on that rainy day.

If you take my daddy, take my daddy, I'll hope you'll be kind
    and true.
If you take my daddy, take my daddy, I'll hope you'll be kind
    and true.
Just like you take him from me somebody's sure to take him
    from you.

You can cheat on me, you can steal on me, you can fool me all
    along.
You can cheat on me, you can steal on me, you can fool me all
    along.
All I ask you, daddy, please don't let me catch you wrong.

'Cause you may do it once, do it twice, but you can't do it all the
    time.
You can do it once, you can do it twice, but you can't do it all the
    time.
You'll put on your last clean shirt when you (grieve that sin kitchen
    of mine).

"Whip It to a Jelly"

There's a new dance that can't be beat, you move most everything 'cept
    your feet.
Called whip it to a jelly, stir it in a bowl.
You just whip it to a jelly if you like good jelly roll.

Folks out west go insane, whip that jelly more everyday, Lord.
Whip it to a jelly and stir it in a bowl.
Now, you whip it to a jelly if you like good jelly roll.

That black gal, long and slim, when she whips it, it to bad jam, Lord.
She whips it to a jelly and stir it in a bowl.
Now, you whip it to a jelly if you like good jelly roll.

I wear my skirt up to my knee and whip that jelly with who I please.
Oh, whip it to a jelly, mmmmmmmmmmmmmm.
Mmmmmmmmmmm, mmmmmmmmm, mmmmmmmmm.

—— Elizabeth Smith ——

Elizabeth Smith recorded the song "Gwine to Have Bad Luck for Seven Years" on Monday, September 6, 1926, on the Victor Label in New York City (Dixon & Godrich). This song fully expresses a woman's need for superstition to explain why trouble and mishaps seem to follow her wherever she goes. She uses the excuse that she stubbed her toe to explain why she no longer has eggs from her hens; in order to understand her misfortunes, she looks to luck.

By reviewing her song "Police Done Tore My Playhouse Down," we may see exactly how helpless a black woman could be against white bureaucracies:

I can't keep open, gotta close the shack.
I can't keep open, gotta close the shack.
No use a grievin', I'm gonna leave this town.
Those cheap ole police done tore my playhouse down.

With no defense against discrimination and no chance for a fair hearing on her "playhouse," she understandably performs songs about superstition such as "Gwine to Have Bad Luck for Seven Years."

"Gwine to Have Bad Luck for Seven Years"

A year ago I broke a looking glass, oh,
A year ago I broke a looking glass.
And since that day, my children give me sass.

117

I stubbed my toe against the kitchen door, oh,
I stubbed my toe against the kitchen door
And now my hen won't lay no eggs no more.

I went to church, sat in the thirteenth row, oh,
I went to church, sat in the thirteenth row.
Next day my landlord said I had to go.

I 'spose there ain't no use of shedding tears, oh,
I 'spose there ain't no use of shedding tears.
I'm gwine to have bad luck for seven years.

——— Mamie Smith ———

Mamie Smith (no relation to Clara or Bessie or Elizabeth) was born on May 26, 1883, in Cincinnati, Ohio, and died on September 16, 1946, in New York, New York (Harris). The first recorded blues song, "Crazy Blues," was made by Mamie Smith in 1920. She performed shows in many theaters on the vaudeville circuit (Harris), and her songs contain many of the typical vaudeville themes.

One of her most popular songs, "Goin Crazy with the Blues," reveals her heartache when her man leaves her. Smith expresses her extreme anxiety over losing her man:

> I'm goin' crazy with the blues since I heard the heartbreakin' news.
> My honey man done thrown me down, now he's spreadin' his sugar
>   everywhere in town.

Another song called "Sweet Virginia Blues" conforms to the vaudeville style by detailing the woman's attitude about rambling; that is, the song expresses a desire to remain stationary rather than to ramble.

Most of the songs sung by Mamie Smith are relatively innocent compared to many of the other songs performed by women blues singers. This could be due to the time frame in which she recorded the songs listed in this anthology, the early 1920s.

"That Thing Called Love"

I worried in my mind.
I worried all the time.
My friend, he told me to say that he was goin' away and stay.

Now I love him deep down in my heart.
But the best of friends must part.
Now, I want somebody please, to cure me of my love disease.
That thing called love will make you sick inside.
That thing called love, money cannot buy.
Will make you sad, will make you glad, will even drive your
    mama mad.
That thing called love has such a funny feelin'.
That thing called love will set your brain a reelin'.
When you're alone, feelin' blue, you're thinkin' 'bout someone
    that don't care for you.
Nobody knows what that thing called love will do.
The thing called love will make you sick inside.
The thing called love that money cannot buy.
Will make you sad, will make you glad, will even drive your
    mama mad.
The thing called love has such a funny feelin'.
That thing called love will set your brain a reelin'.
When you're alone, feelin' blue, you're thinkin' 'bout someone
    that don't care for you.
And nobody knows what the thing called love will do.

"You Can't Keep a Good Man Down"

(I ain't lyin') but it's true
A good man will never do.
It's been said time and again,
He will always win in the end.
So, girls, take my advice and always treat him nice.
You can't keep a good man down, no matter how you try.
Anytime he gets it wrong, he'll find a way by and by
No use tryin' to treat him rough, 'cause he ain't use to that cave
    man stuff.
Kiss him for breakfast, hug him for lunch.
For dinner give him lots of lovin', he's your honey bunch.
'Cause you can't keep a good man down.
He may be down but never out.
I'll tell you now he's a good old scout.

He's always Johnny on the spot.
What it takes to please he sure has got.
So, girls, please bear in mind and always treat him kind.
You can't keep a good man down, no matter how you try.
Anytime he gets it wrong, he'll find a way by and by
No use tryin' to treat him rough, 'cause he ain't use to that cave
    man stuff.
Kiss him for breakfast, hug him for lunch.
For dinner give him lots of lovin', he's your honey bunch.
'Cause you can't keep a good man down.

"Fare Thee Honey Blues"

Now my baby has left me, I don't know what I'll do.
Now every day I miss him, it makes me feel so blue.
I'm leavin' here today and that is why I say,
I'm leavin' town to wear you off my mind.
I been mistreated and I don't mind dyin'
I'll buy me a ticket as long as I ride on.
I'll ride so long you'll think I'm dead and gone.
I'm Alabama bound.

I told him way last spring, when the bluebirds began to sing.
That I was goin' away; that's the word of God, nothin' in the world
    would bring me back.

Now I was slowin' you down. I needed to blow this town.
I'll find me a gun just as long as I'm told,
Shoot that man and get the penalty for it.
Baby, honey, I don't want that song.

If you don't want me, why don't you tell me so?
I can get a friend most anywhere I go.
Every day in the ocean of strangers in the deep blue sea,
I don't want nobody that don't want me.
Don't ya believe me, ya.

"The Road Is Rocky"

Down in (Possum Trot) Mississippi,
Near Cemetery Hill,
There lives a Papa Jenkins,
Who preaches that good will.
But the other day someone stole his drunken gal away.
Yes, they did.
Next Sunday when the meeting was called,
Papa Jenkins got up and bawled.
He said, "The road is rocky but I'm gonna find my way, wait and see.
   I miss my true mama since she left poor me. If she didn't want
   me why did she lie? And the day I see her, that's the day she'll
   die."
The road is rocky but I'm gonna find my way.

Someone said, "Now, Papa Jenkins, you said last Sunday night, we
   should love our neighbor and always treat him right. And you
   said we should always pay back evil deeds with good, yes, you
   did."

The pastor then said "Yes, I agree, but my sermon tonight will be
   about the road is rocky but I'm gonna find my way, wait and
   see. I miss my true mama since she left poor me. If she didn't
   want me, why did she lie? Now the day I see her, that's the day
   she'll die."
The road is rocky but I'm gonna find my way.

Mem'ries of Mammie

When troubles overtake me, Mammie, then my thoughts refer to
   you.
Your image is like the sunshine, Mammie, brighten my darkest
   view.
So you're down below the Mason-Dixon line,
I'm thinkin' 'bout you all the time.
Mem'ries of you will always linger.

When I am feelin' so blue, I often sigh, sometimes cry.
Thinkin' of those days gone by and how you sang that lullaby.
Oh, don't you weep, my honey, don't you cry.
Oh, Lawdy, how I long to see you again
And feel the comfort. (There's no use to carry) on.
I've not forgotten; I can't forget those prayers you used to say night
    and day.
Mem'ries of you will linger with me, Mammie.

Spoken: Mammie, I can see you now. Standing by that old log cabin
    door. Oh, Mammie, I can't forget that good old cornbread and
    cabbage you used to give me. It sure was good. I mean, it was
    good. Mammie, you know that fresh milk from the cow every
    morn' and that good old watermelon, sugar cane and corn. You
    know, Mammie, when we could stand the darkest nights all day
    until the dawn. Believe me, Mammie, them sure were the happy
    days. Mammie, do you remember when Pappie used to take me
    across his lap? Now, I know you can't forget that. And believe me,
    Mammie, he sure was a man that sure could use one more wicked
    spank and I can't forget that.

Sung: I can't forget those things you used to say; they seem to linger
    night and day.
Mem'ries of you will linger with me, Mammie.

"If You Don't Want Me Blues"

My friend and I had a decree.
It seems as though he don't want me.
Every time he sees me, he starts to growl,
He turns the place with him he don't know how.
But my time will come someday, then I'm goin' to him and say,
If you don't want me give me your right hand, not in vain.
I can tell a friend anything by now. Yes I can.
There's a lesson I was always taught, there's plenty of fish in the sea
    and then there was more,
True love cannot be bought.
Do you hear me?
You never miss, you women tell me when I'm right.

You'll never miss your baby till she says goodbye.
You're gonna cry.
Get away from the window, don't you knock at my door.
Got a new baby, don't want you no more.
If you don't want me, why don't you tell me so, And I'll go.
If you don't want me, why don't you tell me so, tell me babe.
I can get a friend anywhere I go, and what is more,
There will be nights you yearn for me and treat me like a ( )
And I know you can count on me. Oh my honey,
If you don't want me, please don't shove me around.
Hear my plea, I'm a good girl now, that will be found in this here
    town.
If you don't want me, tell me to my face.
There's plenty other guys waitin' to take your place.
If you don't want me, why don't you tell me so, and I'll go.

"Lovin' Sam from Alabam'"

Every evenin' 'bout half past eight, you'll see me standin' at my gate.
Waitin' for Sam to come along, he is my man but he done me wrong.
He just won my heart and hand; I'm just wild 'bout my man.
Lovin' is a thing I always need, when he loves, I'm always pleased.
Oh my lovin' Sam, my lovin' man from Alabam', how I love him
    goodness knows,
I love him from his head way down to his toes.
When he loves, he loves so sweet, and at the game, he can't be beat.
I'm crazy 'bout him, can't do without him, I'm wild about him, I
    can't be without my lovin' Sam from Alabam'.

All the time I want to love him.
Rain or shine, I want to hug him.
Monday's kiss always brings me bliss.
Tuesday's smile lasts me, honey, for a while.
Wednesday's hug and Thursday's smackin',
Friday's love don't feel the same.
But when Saturday comes, that is just the best.
Sunday's love is different from the rest.
I'm crazy 'bout his lovin', I want it all the time.
Oh my lovin' Sam, my lovin' man from Alabam', how I love him
    goodness knows,

I love him from his head clean down to his toes.
When he loves, he loves so sweet, and at the game, he can't be beat.
I'm crazy 'bout him, can't be without him, I'm wild about him, I
    can't be without my lovin' Sam from Alabam'.

"Jazzbo Ball"

Listen to the jazzy music down at the jazzbo ball.
Anytime you here it you would rise and fall.
Listen to the piano man moan, listen to the old trombone.
And the funny dancers they call down at the jazzbo ball.

Come dance a rockin' sway lay, then go the other way.
Take your lovin' gal, get right on the sound.
Shake your tambourine, we're playin' for you to fight, so blow, hey
    beau, let's do the right.

If you do the cactus slide with your baby by your side,
Then you break a leg, don't forget to crack the egg.
Dance around the hall, down at the jazzbo ball.

Razor Jim was a conquerin' the figures he disformed.
He wrote some rules and regulations on the wall, that's all.
The first rule was, do the jazzbo glide.
And do it neat and have your babe by your side.
Scratch in the gravel, fall in the dirt, if you do the wrong dance then
    you mustn't come back.
If you send me in here, you walk along the side, if you break them
    rules then we'll cut your hide.

You can use a razor, but don't hurt Jim, rules and regulations and
    Razor Jim.
Come dance around and sway, then go the other way.
Take your lovin' gal, get right on the sound.
Shake your tambourine, we're playin' for you to fight, so blow, hey
    beau, let's do the right.
Then you do the cactus slide with your baby by your side,
Then you break a leg, don't forget to crack the egg.
Dance around the hall, down at the jazzbo ball.

"What Have I Done"

A rollin' stone never gathers any moss.
That's what the old folks say.
When I'm gone, you'll see that you've lost your little darling baby.
One word that I wish to say before I go away.
Tell me, dearie, what have I done?
You have mistreated me for some other woman.
Just as sure as the berries grow on the vine
You're going to wilt someday, then you will mourn.
Why can't you love me in December as you did in May?
Don't you know I've always let you have your way?
You're like flower kissed with dew, I found an angel when I found
     you.
Now tell me baby, what have I done?
Why can't you love me in December as you did in May?
Don't you know I've always let you have your way?
You're like flower kissed with dew, I found an angel when I found you.
Now tell me baby, what have I done?

"Frankie Blues"

Frankie was a good girlie to everyone she knew.
She had some trouble with her sweetie, which made her feel so blue.
She packed up real quick for a trip and said, "I'm leavin' here, honey
     dear."

He called me the next day. She left and this is what he had to say.
I'm worried now, ain't gonna be worried long, no I ain't.
I miss good Frankie, since she been gone, yes I do.
She went away, I know she done me wrong.
Now I'm weepin' like a willow tree, ever since that Frankie went
     away from me.
Where she's gone, I do not know; she's been seen in Baltimore.
I will pay every penny and more if you will find dear Frankie, Lord.
I been to 'Frisco, I've gone to Halifax, tryin' to find Frankie and
     bring her back.
So, I'm tryin', please Frankie, you're mine.
Someone's hurt, please Frankie, Lord.
Please, you will give a poor heart a week.

If in the end she threw me down, now she packed away with Henry
    Brown.
So I'm cryin' that dear Frankie, you're mine.
I tell you, now I'm weepin' like a willow tree, ever since that Frankie
    went away from me.
Where she's gone, I do not know; she's been seen in Baltimore.
I will pay every penny and more if you will find dear Frankie, Lord.
I been to 'Frisco, I've gone to Halifax, tryin' to find Frankie and
    bring her back.
So I'm cryin' that dear Frankie, you're mine."

"U Need Some Loving Blues"

I went to see the doctor today, to see what he had to say.
Something must be wrong, I'm worried all day long.
He said I had a love attack, I must get my baby back.
He felt my pulse and right away this is what he had to say,

You need some lovin' when you feel bad, you need some lovin' to
    make you real glad. You need some lovin' when you feel blue,
    you need someone to talk to, baby, and talk to you.
Some sweet caressing every night and day. Someone to love you in
    that old fashioned way. Hit you with all of that power. Repeat
    this sixty times every hour. You need some lovin', must have
    it all of the time, to ease your mind.

You need some lovin' when you feel bad, you need some lovin' to
    make you real glad. You need some lovin' when you feel blue,
    you need someone to talk to, baby, and talk to you.
Some sweet caressing every night and day. Someone to love you in
    that old fashioned way. Hit you with all of that power. Repeat
    this sixty times every hour. You need some lovin', must have
    it all of the time, to ease your mind.

"The Lure of the South"

See that steamboat comin', comin' round the bend.
All you brothers and sisters shout Amen.

Get on board, little children, get on board, little children, get on board
    little children, there's room for many aboard.
I'm feelin' lonesome, homesick, and blue for my sunny southland.
When nights are fallin', I feel the southland callin'.
I'm headin' home as soon as I can, to my sunny southland.
When my luck starts breakin', there's a trip I'm takin'.
Well, the cotton pickers work in crews.
And the field workers you'll hear their tunes.
I tell you, that's the lure of the south.

When you hear the steamboat whistle blow, and the lazy water's
    churnin' below,
I tell you, that's the lure of the south.

Everything that I made since I started to roam,
Everything I would trade to be back south at home.
When you hear birds singin' all year round,
And your feet are feelin' homeward bound,
I tell you, that's the lure of the south.

Workin' in the cotton fields beneath the sun,
Dancin' in the moonlight when the work is done.
Singin' happy songs and always havin' fun.
Just like in paradise.
Where my man is waitin' at the cabin door,
Back strummin' hummin' on the river shore,
I will say I'm happy when I'm south once more,
Beneath the southern sky.
Well, the cotton pickers work in crews.
And the field workers, you'll hear their tunes.
I tell you, that's the lure of the south.

When you hear the steamboat whistle blow, and the lazy water's
    churnin' below,
I tell you, that's the lure of the south.

Everything that I made since I started to roam,
Everything I would trade to be back south at home.
When you hear birds singin' all year round,
And your feet are feelin' homeward bound,
I tell you, that's the lure of the south.

─── Trixie Smith ───

Trixie Smith (no relation to Clara, Bessie, Elizabeth or Mamie), otherwise known as Tesse Ames or Bessie Lee, was born in 1895, in Atlanta, Georgia, and died on September 21, 1943, in New York, New York (Harris). Smith toured and worked in many theaters on the vaudeville circuit.

Perhaps the most thorough account of Trixie Smith's life appears in Daphne Harrison's *Black Pearls*, wherein Harrison informs her readers of the many ups and downs of Smith's career. Harrison reports that Smith recorded less than "fifty sides between 1923 and 1939" (245), and explains that "since much of the material that Trixie sang is rather vacuous, her lightweight voice does not make the material particularly memorable" (245). Harrison also reveals that she concluded work with Paramount in 1925 and "faded into obscurity except for a brief return to the club scene in New York in the late 1930s" (245).

From one of her most popular songs entitled "Freight Train Blues," we may infer that Trixie Smith, like Mamie Smith, regards rambling as a distasteful attribute of manhood. In this song, Smith says, "Got the freight train blues, that boxcar's on my mind. I'm gonna leave this town 'cause my man is gone on time." Smith relays contempt for the freight train that takes her man away from her to serve time for a crime.

"I Don't Know and I Don't Care Blues"

Sally Snow was a carefree gal with a heart like a piece of lead.
She had a man, beat up too long but not no more she says.
He packed his grip and went away with blood in both his eyes.

129

A friend asked Sally where he went and fully she replied.
I don't know and I don't care where my lovin' Daddy's gone.
He should have gone long ago, I'd like to know what he's waiting on.
Sweet mama Sally's like a four month wind,
Changes every now and then.
She found it really pays you in the end to make a little change in
    men.
So, I don't know and I don't care which way my daddy's gone.
If you love a man he'll treat you like a dog,
If you don't, he'll hop around you like a frog.
So, I don't know and I don't care where my lovin' Daddy's gone.
I ain't seen the man that I can't stand to lose.
It's 'cause I keep the don't know and the don't care blues.
Now, I don't know and I don't care where my lovin' daddy's gone.

"Sorrowful Blues"

If you catch me stealin', I don't mean no harm.
If you catch me stealin', I don't mean no harm.
It's a mark in my family, it must be carried on.

I've got nineteen men and I want one more.
I've got nineteen men and I want one more.
When I get that one more, I'll let that nineteenth go.

I'm goin' to tell you, daddy, like the Chinaman told the Jew.
I'm goin' to tell you, daddy, like the Chinaman told the Jew.
If you don't likey me, me sure don't likey you.

It's hard to love another woman's man.
I say, It's hard to love another woman's man.
You can't get him when you want him, you gotta catch him when
    you can.

Have you ever seen peaches grow on a sweet potato vine?
Have you ever seen peaches grow on a sweet potato vine?
Just step in my back yard and take a peek at mine.

—— Victoria Spivey ——

Victoria Spivey was born on October 15, 1906, in Houston, Texas, and died on October 3, 1976, in New York City (Harris). While Spivey did travel on the vaudeville circuit, she had the chance to play in the tougher men's clubs with renowned male blues singers such as Blind Lemon Jefferson and Lonnie Johnson (Harris).

It may be that performing in these clubs caused Spivey to sing songs which appear more crude in nature; songs such as "New Black Snake Blues" contain lyrics which are expressly geared towards sex. Furthermore, in "Detroit Moan," Spivey refers to prostitution without trying to cover up the act when she says, "I been workin' Hassen Street, nobody seems to treat me right." In her other songs, Spivey talks about the use of drugs in "Dopehead Blues," the ails of tuberculosis in "T.B.'s Got Me," and the passions that lead a woman to murder her man after he has cheated on her in "Murder in the First Degree." While some of her songs conform to the vaudeville style, Spivey boldly stretches its limits with lyrics that would normally be considered too rude for a theater audience.

"Detroit Moan"

Detroit's a cold, cold place and I ain't got a dime to my name.
Detroit's a cold, cold place and I ain't got a dime to my name.
I would go to the poor house but, Lord, you know I'm ashamed.

I been workin' Hassen Street, nobody seem to treat me right.
I been workin' Hassen Street, nobody seem to treat me right.
I can make it in the daytime but, Lord, these cold, cold nights.

131

Well, I'm tired of eatin' chili and I can't eat beans no more.
Yes, I'm tired of eatin' chili and I can't eat beans no more.
People hurt my feelings, Lord, from dusk to dawn.

I've got to leave Detroit if I have to flag number ninety-four.
I'm gonna leave Detroit if I have to flag number ninety-four.
And if I ever get back home, I ain't never comin' to Detroit no more.

"Arkansas Road Blues"

I got my sing sang and now I'm goin' back
Because I've got those Arkansas blues.
But I ain't gonna travel that State road by my, mmmmmm,
    by myself.
I ain't gonna travel that State Road by myself.
If I don't take my baby, I sure won't have nobody else.

But when he was arrested and put in that mean ole, ummm,
    mean ole jail.
When he were arrested and put in that mean ole jail,
I were the only person to try and earn his bail.

Ahhh, ayyyy, ayyyy, ayyyyy, ahhhhhh, baby why'd you let me go?
Daddy, if you don't want me there are plenty more.

"Don't Trust Nobody Blues"

I don't trust nobody, but the good Lord above.
I don't trust nobody, baby, but the good Lord above.
And aside of my mother, there's nobody else I love.

Men will love you and fool you, make you spend all your dough.
Love you and fool you, make you spend all your dough.
After they get what they want, why, they don't like you no more.

Drunken friend, oh, and sick too, waiting for a chance, to double
    cross you.
mmmmmmm, this ain't no place for me.
Well I'm goin' out the country, I mean across the deep blue sea.

Oh, friendship ain't no good, that's why I'm hittin' that long, long
    trail.
Oh, friendship ain't no good, that's why I'm hittin' that long, long
    trail.
Because to fool with my money, mama don't mind goin' to jail.

Here I lay after midnight, drinkin' my fool self to sleep.
Lay after midnight, drinkin' my fool self to sleep.
While that low down man of mine is tryin' to make his four day creep.

"The Alligator Pond Went Dry"

Folks, I'm tellin' you something that I saw with my own eyes,
Back at the pond one day.
The ole alligator was teachin' his babies to do the Georgie cry.
Then I heard one of them say,
There's a social but the alligator pond's goin' dry.
Yes, it is a social but the alligator pond's goin' dry.
Now, ole Mr. Alligator, he got way back.
He say, look out children now, I'm gonna cut my back.
Oh, it was a social, but the alligator pond went dry.
Oh, it musta been a social, but the alligator pond went dry.
Oh, it musta been a social, for the alligator pond to go dry.
Now, ole Miss Alligator, she got real hot.
She said we're gonna have this function whether there is water or not.
Oh, it was a social when the alligator pond went dry.

Now, if you don't believe what I'm sayin', ask ole Alligator Jack.
Wasn't a drop of water in the pond when he got back.
It was a social when the alligator pond went dry.

"Murder in the First Degree"

Well, I'm layin here in this jailhouse scared as any fool can be,
Yes, I'm layin here in this jailhouse scared as any fool can be.
I believe they're gonna hang me from what my lawyer say to me.

My man got runnin' around with a woman he know I can't stand.
My man got runnin' around with a woman he know I can't stand.
That's why I got my gun and got rid of one triflin' man.

I scrub them pots and kettles, I washed and ironed the white folks'
    clothes.
I scrub them pots and kettles, I washed and ironed the white folks'
    clothes.
He got it like I make him, I kill him, Judge, that's all I know.

Judge, if you would've killed your woman and had to come before
    me,
If you'd a killed a woman who trifled and had to come before me,
I'd send her to the jailhouse and, Judge, let you go free.

I said I ain't done nothin' but kill a man, what belongs to me.
I said I ain't done nothin' but kill a man, what belongs to me.
And yet they got me charged with murder in the first degree.

"Give It to Him"

To my fullest satisfaction I have learned that men like action.
But that doesn't mean that you should go and cheat on me.
I am one who (penalizes) even when and if it's speaking pleasure,
And I go for givin' my men what a man should need.
Girl, don't get the wrong impression, men don't care for much
    discretion.
Don't hold out your best assertion, give it to him.
That machinery must have oilin', meat keeps longer wrapped
    in foilin',
Love itself ain't free from spoilin', give it to him.

Have to give away a fortune may not be so bad.
Give him credit for the bunch of fun they must've had.
Men have taught to gamble a lot, they want all the love you got.
And they'd rather have it hot, so give it to him.
Men don't care for lots of chatter, and I know, gal, it just don't matter.
Don't care if it's gonna splatter, give it to him.
Now, if you are plump or slender, long as you are sweet and tender,
Let your man know you surrender, let him have it.

You may be a kick at fishin', men don't get a bite.
So get catchin', and get cookin', fix your bait just right.
Gals, this must be understood, don't love like a chunk of wood.
Make your man know that it's good, make him like it.
Never let a man (employ) if he has a lot in store,
If he wants a little bit more, give it to him.
If he's got it don't make him blow it, if you got 'em bigger show 'im,
     let him also know you know it, shake 'em at 'im.
Why, see old Patrick, give it to him, after pick my dad, why she's
     Exhibit A through U and everything's been had.
Every man that I can find, love to know that he is mine. Even when
     I'm too tired, I throw it at 'em.

"I Can't Last Long"

Ohhh, Ohhhh, yes I'm sinkin', sinkin', sinkin' down below my grave.
Well, I had a good time, but Lord, how I done paid.

Well, the risin' sun ain't gonna shine no more.
Said the risin' sun ain't gonna shine no more.
'Cause it's dark and dreary everywhere I go.

Well, the light in my room even refuse to shine.
Ah, the light in my room even refuse to shine.
If my baby don't come back I know I'll be doin' time.

Because, oh, I can't stand no more.
Mmmm, I can't stand no more.
Well, he quit me for my best friend and don't come to see me no more.

Tell all my good friends, 'cause I know I can't last long.
Tell all my good friends, I know I can't last long.
Please don't you wait, for I'll be dead and gone.

Mmmmmm, ohhhhhh, mmmmmmmm, mmmmmmmmmmmm
Please don't you wait, 'cause I know I'll be dead and gone.

"Black Snake Blues"

Johnny blowed just like it ain't never been blowed before.

Got a black snake been stuck in my rattle.
Hear me cry, Lord, I mean it.
Some black snake been stuck in my (rattle stone).
You can tell by that I ain't gonna stay here long.

'Cause in my lace pajama flesh began to crawl.
My lace pajama flesh began to crawl.
Bet you my last dollar there's another woman kickin' in my stall.

Oh, I ain't gonna tell you no more.
Oh, I ain't gonna tell you no more.
Stay from my window, don't knock at my back door.

I'd rather be catfish swimmin' in that deep blue,
Lord, beneath a submarine behind a floatin' boat.
I'd rather be a catfish, Lord, in that deep blue sea.
Should a stayed in Texas, feel like what they wanted to do for me.

Oh, I ain't gonna tell you no more.
Oh, been in that deep blue sea.
Should a stayed in Texas, feel like what they wanted to do for me.

If you meet any black snakes just carry me to his gate.
But learn from my mistake, ain't hard for me to take.
It's a mean black snake that's doin' me this a way.
If I ever go back south, I'm goin' there to stay.

"Christmas Mornin' Blues"

Spoken: Bless you there, woman.
Spoken: For what, not a child or chicken in the yard?

Woke up Christmas mornin', went out to get the mornin' mail.
I woke up Christmas mornin', went out to get the mornin' mail.
A letter sent from Georgia, the postman marked it last from jail.

In a mean ole jailhouse, 'cause he broke the Georgia law.
In a mean ole jailhouse, 'cause he broke them Georgia laws.
New Year's he won't be here, 'cause death will be his Santa Claus.

My man so deep in trouble the white folks couldn't get him free.
My man so deep in trouble the white folks couldn't get him free.
He stole a hog, the charge was murder in the first degree.

I ain't never had a Christmas with trouble like this before.
I ain't never had a Christmas with trouble like this before.
Them bells is my death bells and hard luck knockin' at my door.

Next Christmas I won't be here to get this bad bunch of news.
I won't be here to get this bunch of bad news.
It's written on my tombstone I died with Christmas mornin' blues.

"How Do You Do It That Way?"

Have you ever had a feelin' that someone would come a stealin' you?
If you have, it's not so bad unless you find that it is all untrue.
Takes a good girl to keep her man, some can't do it, others can.
I'm no chump, but I would jump, if I could find someone that kinda
    likes me too.
Oh, when the river runs, flowers are bloomin' in May.
And if you get good business, how do you do it that way?
Street walkin' women, they're all happy and gay.
But I'm never happy, how do you get that way?

I want a man to be near because he bring good cheer.
But the men don't like me, they don't seem to care.
Now they can come and go, to and fro everyday.
But I can't make 'em like me like you do it that way.

Now if you want something good you must knock on wood.
Just get a good man to look up under your hood.
And when the rooster and the hen go to the barn to play,
Oh, the hen has chickens, how do they do it that way?

"I'll Keep Sittin' on It If I Can't Sell It"

If I can't sell it, keep sittin' on it, before I give it away.
You've got to buy it, don't care how much you want it, I mean just
    what I say.

Just feel that nice old bottom bit, no wear or tear,
I really hate to part with such a lovely chair.
If I can't sell it, keep sittin' on it, before I give it away.
If I can't sell it, I'll keep sittin' on it, before I give it away.
You've got to buy it, don't care how much you want it, I mean just
what I say.
When you want something good you've got to spend your jack.
I'll guar'ntee you will never want your money back.
If I can't sell it, I'll keep sittin' on it, before I give it away.

If I can't sell it, I'll keep sittin' on it, before I give it away.
You've got to buy it, don't care how much you want it, I mean just
what I say.
When you want something good you've got to spend your jack.
I'll guar'ntee you will never want your money back.
If I can't sell it, I'll keep sittin' on it, before I give it away.
Oh, daddy, yes before I give it away.

——— Priscilla Stewart ———

Priscilla Stewart recorded both "A Little Bit Closer" and "I Want to See My Baby" in December 1928 on the Paramount label in Chicago (Dixon & Godrich). These two songs are different from many of the other women's blues lyrics portrayed thus far. "A Little Bit Closer" is very upbeat in tempo, and the lyrics to this song reveal that her man is not mistreating at all, which is a rather unusual theme for a woman's blues song. Furthermore, in "I Want to See My Baby," Stewart actually admits to being the mistreater instead of being the victim of abuse; she claims she has made her spouse a victim of wrongdoings.

While little information about Priscilla Stewart's life may be found, Harrison discovered that she performed under the Paramount label and describes her as one of the "others who thrived briefly over the decade [1930s]" (247), yet attained little fame.

"A Little Bit Closer"

A little bit closer, a little bit closer to me.
I really enjoy it, a little bit closer to me.

Earth and sky are close together.
The shore is always close to the sea.
But my daddy gets closer, a little bit closer to me.

Talk about your lovin' daddy, I got one that's too bad.
Ooh, I've got a new sensation like I never had.
When he puts his arms around me and his lips touch mine,
He just thrills me through and through and I can't help but whine.

A little bit closer, a little bit closer to me.
I really enjoy it, a little bit closer to me.

Earth and sky are close together.
The shore is always close to the sea.
But my daddy gets closer, a little bit closer to me.
A little bit closer, a little bit closer to me.
I really enjoy it, a little bit closer to me.

"I Want to See My Baby"

I want to see my baby, my baby I treated so wrong.
I want to see my baby, my baby I treated so wrong.
I want to see my baby, 'cause I been in jail so long.

My baby says you're gonna be sorry, you're gonna be sorry some day.
Ah, you're gonna be sorry some day.
'Cause you don't know how I miss you when you are so far away.

So many have been lonesome, so many have the blues,
I want to see my baby so bad I put on my walkin' shoes.
I want to see my baby, my baby I treated so wrong.
I want to see my baby, 'cause I been in jail so long.

I wonder who's been givin' you lovin', you lovin' since I been gone.
Ah, eee, since I been gone.
I want to see my baby, my baby I treated so wrong.

——— Hociel Thomas ———

Hociel Thomas was born on July 10, 1904, in Houston, Texas, and died on August 22, 1952, in Oakland, California (Harris). Thomas was the niece of another great female blues singer, Sippie Wallace, and she lived with her aunt when she was 20 (Harris). Other biographical information about Hociel Thomas discloses that she was in a fight with her sister that caused her to go blind and resulted in her sister's death (Harris).

In fact, her blues song entitled "Deep Water Blues" portrays her tendency toward violence when she believes she is in an unfair situation: "Catch you in deep water, tear your eyeballs out." While blues songs are normally considered a catharsis for releasing unfavorable feelings, they may actually have precipitated violence in some instances.

According to Harrison, Hociel had a younger brother named Hersal Thomas, and Hociel, Hersal and Wallace created a trio that performed often (120).

"Deep Water Blues"

Nobody knows what's on my troubling mind.
My man abuses me 'round and now I feel like dyin'.
I can never tell when my man's gonna throw me down.
'Cause he's mean and evil every time he comes around.

You're trying to do right, baby, you want to right yourself.
If you don't do no better I'm gonna get somebody else.
'Cause there's trouble, trouble, trouble everywhere I go.
When I wake up every morning, trouble standin' in my door.

141

Now you must want your mama to lay down and die for you.
Layin' down's all right but dying will never do.
I'm gonna tell you, baby, like the tadpole told a trout,
Catch you in deep waters, tear your eyeballs out.

"Lonesome Hours"

Let me tell you what my sweet man done one day.
Oh, let me tell you what my sweet man done one day.
He broke my heart just to pass the time away.

My man was cute and wore a (shoe size) number two.
My man was cute and wore a (shoe size) number two.
But he once up and left me with a woman looks just like you.

The reason I love him, I stole him from my best friend.
Lord, the reason I love him, I stole him from my best friend.
But she got lucky and stole him back again.

Ever since he left me, I been wondering what must I do.
Ever since he left me, I been wondering what must I do.
'Cause these lonesome hours always keep me blue.

—— Sippie Wallace ——

Beulah Wallace, most commonly referred to as Sippie Wallace, was born on November 11, 1898, in Houston, Texas (Harris), and died in 1986 (Herzhaft). Wallace had a direct influence on Bonnie Raitt, and the two recorded an album together on the Atlantic label in 1983 (Herzhaft).

Sippie Wallace toured on the vaudeville circuit. One of her many hits, "Suitcase Blues," shows the typical attitude toward rambling held by women blues performers on that circuit. In this song, she proclaims her animosity toward rambling: "But I'm scared to go down that big road myself," yet she plans to carry through with her plan to ramble, which is evident when she says, "I hear the whistle blowin', I believe I'll be on my way. Give me my suitcase, I'll see you some ole day." While Wallace detests the thought of leaving her home, she feels she must leave her mistreating man. Wallace's "Suitcase Blues" follows the traditional style of vaudeville in that the lyrics portray both her contempt of rambling and the sheer necessity of doing so.

Wallace was one of the female blues singers who retained her popularity; she recorded albums well into the 1980s. In fact, her album "A Mighty Tight Woman" was nominated for the 1983 Grammy award (Harrison).

For a more thorough biography of Sippie Wallace's life see Daphne Harrison's *Black Pearls*, chapter 4, entitled "Up the Country and Still Singing the Blues: Sippie Wallace" (113-145).

"Jack of Diamond Blues"

Jack of Diamonds, you appear to be my friend.
Jack of Diamonds, you appear to be my friend
But gambling is gonna be our end.

143

You stole all my money and you put up all my clothes.
You stole all my money and put up all my clothes.
And you came home broke and tried to put me out of doors.

Now I traveled the whole wide world through.
Now I traveled the whole round world through.
There is nothin' in this world I found that pleases you.

I loved Jack of Diamonds but he was a cruel man.
I loved Jack of Diamonds but he was a cruel man.
He would place down those bet cards and his game was ole coon's
    can.

"A Jealous Woman Like Me"

My man got up, I mean he's up, and he is feelin' kinda wrong.
My man got up this mornin' feeling kinda wrong.
Daddy dreamed last night someone had took his woman and gone.

Tell me, oh, please tell me what's on your worried mind.
Tell me baby, why can't you love me too?
You love everybody, what is wrong with you?
'Cause a man like you, I think I'm just about to lose.

A jealous woman like me ain't never got no words.
A jealous woman like me ain't never got no words.
'Cause I'm always listening to something that I've heard.

"The Mail Train Blues"

My sweet man's done gone and left me sad.
He makes me feel just like goin' right to the bed.
I need lovin' everyday, I sure miss him plenty since he went away.
I feel just like I could go to my bedroom and cry.
Feel just like I could go somewhere and die.

Anyone can understand I've got to find that loving man.
I'm going to have me a ticket when the mail train rolls around.
I don't care where it goes to, my man must be found.

I wanna (bench hop), don't stop.
Don't care if there's an engine in it or not.
I'm gonna ride on that mail train, till I've run my daddy down.

I wanna (bench hop), don't stop.
Don't care if there's an engine in it or not.
I'm gonna ride on that mail train, till I've run my man down.

"I Feel Good"

When I was a kid, I knew a plea.
I plead with everything that I see.
I don't do them foolish things no more.
'Cause that don't bring me any dough.
Now, there are lots of gals going round.
They have had fun in many ole town.
No, no that stuff never bothers me.
'Cause I feel good as good can be.
I feel good, I mean, I love my baby.
I feel good, and I don't mean maybe.
I love my man, I love my child.
Folks, I got to stop and rest a little while.

I feel good, every way about me.
I don't have to sulk.
If you only knew what my man's got,
I'll tell you right now he's got a lot.
Folks, you know I sure feel good.
Folks, I got to stop and rest a little while.
I feel good, every way about me.
I don't have to sulk.
I ain't gonna tell you what I have got.
My man loves me better than a hog loves slop.
Folks, I sure feel good.

"A Man for Every Day of the Week"

I am feeling mean and blue, evil as can be.
'Cause me and my seven men, we all can't agree.

They keep me bothered night and day, tryin' to keep 'em fed.
But the money I get from all my men, don't worry I'm bound to
    spend.
Now, my Monday man he works on Fourth and Main.
My Tuesday man gives me my spendin' change.
My Wednesday man buys my hats and shoes.
My Thursday man don't care what I do.
Now, my Friday man he buys my home brewed beer.
My Saturday man went dancing (dancing here).
My Sunday man he dress so nice and neat.
He's a nice sweet man I'm always eager to meet.

I've got a regular man for each morn' I rise.
Bring me good earned money each day past five.
I want you all to learn to make your ends all meet.
And every night a good man for every day of the week.

"Dead Drunk Blues"

Give me Houston, Detroit is not my craze.
Oh, give me Houston, Detroit is not my craze.
'Cause when I'm dry, I can drink whiskey, just me.

Whiskey, whiskey is the folks' downfall.
Oh, whiskey is the folks' downfall.
But if I don't drink whiskey, I ain't no good at all.

Have you ever been drunk, slept in all of your clothes?
Have you ever been drunk, slept in all of your clothes?
And when you woke up you found that you were out of dough.

I'm gonna get drunk, papa, just one more time.
Oh, daddy, just one more time.
'Cause when I'm drunk, nothin' don't worry my mind.

—— Lorraine Walton ——

Lorraine Walton sings the song "If You're a Viper" with great enthusiasm, and this song fully elaborates on the need for marijuana to ease the pain of a miserable social environment. The term "viper," which stands for a marijuana cigarette, becomes the saving grace for a person who doesn't have the money to pay the rent. In fact, the desire for marijuana is so intense that Walton begins the song, "I dreamed about a reefer five feet long." Thoughts of marijuana even invade her dreams at night.

"If You're a Viper"

Dreamed about a reefer five foot long, mighty big but not too strong.
You be high but not for long.
If you're a viper.
'Cause I'm the queen of everything.
I got to be high before I can swing.
Light a tea and let it be.
If you're a viper.
When your throat gets dry, you know you're high.
Everything is dandy and you truck on down to the candy store.
Bust your cunk on peppermint candy.
Then you know your brown body's spent.
You don't care if you don't pay rent.
Sky's high but so am I, if you're a viper.

Dreamed about a reefer five foot long, mighty big but not too strong.
You be high but not for long.

If you're a viper.
'Cause I'm the queen of everything.
I got to be high before I can swing.
Light a tea and let it be.
If you're a viper.
When your throat gets dry, you know you're high.
Everything is dandy and you truck on down to the candy store.
Bust your cunk on peppermint candy.
Then you know your brown body's spent.
You don't care if you don't pay rent.
Sky's high but so am I, if you're a viper.

—— Georgia White ——

Georgia White's "Walkin' the Street" contains lyrics similar to Rainey's "Hustlin' Blues." While no biographical information on White may be found, it seems that Rainey had an influence on White, considering the similarity in theme and music between the two songs. Both discuss the troubles of prostitution as a means of survival; in both songs it is raining while the women try to turn a trick, both try to make money and cannot, and both complain about the unworthiness of their men.

"Walkin' the Street"

Stood on the corner till my feet got soakin' wet.
Stood on the corner till my feet got soakin' wet.
These are the words I said to each and every man I met.

If you ain't got a dollar, give me a lousy dime.
If you ain't got a dollar, give me a lousy dime.
I've got to beg and steal to please that man of mine.

My feets are blistered just from walkin' these lonesome streets.
My feets are blistered just from walkin' these lonesome streets.
I been walkin' all night like a police on his beat.

Wait a minute Mr. Mister, give me a cigarette.
Wait a minute Mr. Mister, give me a cigarette.
Stop your car, let me in, I've got what you should get.

I've got these street walkin' blues, I ain't got no time to lose.
I've got these street walkin' blues, I ain't got no time to lose.
I've got to make six dollars just to buy my man a pair of shoes.

— Margaret Whitmire —

Margaret Whitmire recorded "T'ain't a Cow in Texas" and "That Thing's Done Been Put on Me" on October 5, 1927, on the Brunswick label in Chicago (Dixon & Godrich). Both songs talk about the trials of love, and "That Thing's Done Been Put on Me" uncovers the superstitious belief in witch doctors who can cast spells on others. In this song, Whitmire explains her fear that her "daddy" has put a spell on her, probably because he found out that she has other men in her life.

"T'ain't a Cow in Texas"

Oh, baby, please be good to me,
I'm mad just like a willow tree.
Throw your arms around me, hold me till I yell soowee.
I love you like a monkey loves to climb a coconut tree.
If I don't, t'ain't a cow in Texas.

You got me tied into a knot.
I'll give you anything I got.
And if I ain't got it, I'll go and find it just for you.
I love you honey, love you, love you like you want me to.
If I don't, t'ain't a cow in Texas.

I'd just as soon to be in jail,
Or swallowed whole by some old whale.
Baby, if you leave me, I'll break apart a Ferris wheel.
If I don't love you, honey, Boston never had a bee.
If I don't, t'ain't a cow in Texas.

I'd walk into a lion's den?
I'd even fight a (lion).
Honey, if I catch you foolin' with another woman,
There'll be some lonesome music but you'll never hear the band.
If I don't, t'ain't a cow in Texas.

"That Thing's Done Been Put on Me"

I goes to bed in middream; I burns up with the heat.
I'm naked from my eyebrows to the bottom of my feet.
I've three men in my head; I'm as crazy as a fool can be.
I believe to my soul, that doggone thing's been put on me.

You ask if he's a man, my friend, don't be no fool.
He cert'nly couldn't feed no woman, couldn't hardly feed no mule.
I'm so crazy in my head, I could run and jump into the sea.
I believe to my soul, that man's done put that thing on me.

Girls, there never was no man that could treat me like he do.
And, partner, if you had 'im, he do the same to you.
I don't know but I believe, he's done put somethin' in my tea.
From the way that I feel, he's put that doggone thing on me.

He goes away and leaves me and comes back full of gin.
And tells me what to do if I simply ask him where he's been.
I done know he's a trifler, but I'm crazy 'bout him as can be.
That's why I believe he's put that doggone thing on me.

Folks, when that thing's on you, you don't even feel alone.
You're just so doggone crazy, you'll fight your ma and pa.
I've tried to quit this man, but I just can't let him be.
That's why I know to my soul, he's done put that doggone thing
    on me.

——— Edna Winston ———

Edna Winston's "I Got a Mule to Ride," "Mama's Gonna Drop Your Curtain," "Pail in My Hand," and "Peepin' Jim" were all recorded on Tuesday, November 23, 1926, on the Victor label in New York City (Dixon & Godrich). "Way After One and My Daddy Ain't Come Home Yet," "Joogie Blues," and "Ever After On" were recorded on Wednesday, February 16, 1928, also on the Victor label in New York City (Dixon & Godrich).

While not much is known about Winston, it is probable that she too toured the vaudeville circuit, as her songs follow the vaudeville tradition. For example, in "Mama's Gonna Drop Your Curtain," Winston politely discusses how she will kill her spouse if she finds out he is cheating on her: "I'll touch my blade if you try to get too bold, I ain't gonna take no time to get you told." Although Winston implies a definite threat, she is not overly boisterous or rude about it in any way. Much like vaudeville singers mask their discussion of sex, Winston politely refers to murder.

"I Got a Mule to Ride"

Did you ever, ever, feel like you sittin' in the brand new hay?
Wake up in the mornin' and you feel so bad.
Thinkin' 'bout your baby and your heart so sad.

I got a mule to ride and I can't be satisfied.
The house catch on fire, throw my trunk outside.
If you try to leave me, I've got a mule to ride.

I had to leave New York, walkin' and talkin' to myself.
I had to leave New York, walkin' and talkin' to myself.
The man I love was crazy 'bout somebody else.

Hey, hey, hey, hey, hey, hey.
Hey, hey, hey, hey, hey, hey.
I've got the blues so bad I don't know what to do.

"Mama's Gonna Drop Your Curtain"

Hey, hot papa, don't you try to be so flip.
Say, hot papa, so you givin' your lips.
And if I catch you foolin' around, I'm cert'nly gonna lay you down.
The first gal I catch you kissin' will be the last gal you ever kiss.
Just like the sighs you're missin', missin' like you never was missed.
Just drop your curtain, say you're a married man, babe.
For your mama's gonna drop your curtain and stuff it in your face,
    but you won't know it.
I commit a crime, if you try to get too bold.
I ain't gonna take no time to get you told.
I touch my blade and cut away your happiness.
For the first gal I catch you kissin' will be the last gal you ever kiss.
For the first gal I catch you kissin' will be the last gal you ever kiss.
Just like the sighs you're missin', missin' like you never was missed.
Just drop your curtain, say you're a married man, babe.
Or your mama's gonna drop your curtain and stuff it in your face,
    but you won't know it.
I'll commit a crime if you try to get too bold.
I ain't gonna take no time to get you told.
I take my blade and cut away your happiness.
For the letter you get will be the last one you ever get.

"Pail in My Hand"

Blues have got me all the live long day.
I'm disgusted, feel like running away.

Just seems like there's no place to go.
Seems like all the folks I know are livin' in the same boat that I row.
This scrubbin' has got my goat.
For a little more I'll cut my throat.
Got a pail in my hand, on my knees all day long.

If I had a good man, I wouldn't do him wrong.
Ain't got no chance to even be bad.
So full of ambition, it makes me sad.
Lordy, Lord, what can I do?
Got a pail in my hand, (washin' britches) all day long.

If I had a good man I wouldn't do him wrong.
Only one thing I regret.
Everybody thinks that I'm all wet,
Got a pail in my hand, on my knees all day long.

Only one thing I regret,
Everybody thinks I'm all wet,
Got a pail in my hand, on my knees all day long.

"Peepin' Jim"

Let me tell you about Jim; let me tell you about Jim.
Jim's got ways like the devil,
It must be more than him.
Everybody well knows he's runnin' me down.
Ain't no use of talkin' he's sure wouldn't even know how.
Jim's got ways like a railroad sort of man.
Always got his grips right in his hand.
You can't tell if he's in or out.
He's always somewhere 'round about.
I ain't gonna spend my days with Peepin' Jim.

Peepin', peepin', it sort of make him sad.
If he keeps on peepin', he'll be sorry that he had.
I'll let him see another peek, hug and kiss me, oh, so sweet.
The way I do might feel a bit too bad.
The other day, I went out for a stroll.
The other day, I went out for a stroll.

When I came back from where I been, there was Jim peeping in.
He's been on his knees lookin' through the keyhole.

"Way After One and My Daddy Ain't Come Home Yet"

I had a nice papa, a pretty good papa, but I'm puzzled now.
'Cause my papa had a little roamer, then we had a bout.
I'm wonderin' if he's mad, or if he's took his vows.
He grabbed his hat and slammed the door, curtain without a bower.
Way after one, papa ain't come back yet.

He thinks it fun, I'm sorry we ever met.
Oh, the devil's busy, that man's got me dizzy.
Oh, my name is hazy.
I believe I'm goin' crazy.
He went out then I'm going to stay.
For he only spoke them words in play.
Way after Monday, Tuesday, Wednesday, Thursday, Friday, Saturday,
    Sunday.
Way after one, my daddy ain't come home yet.

January's gone, February's gone, he marched away.
June, July and August, I left out April and May.
September, October, November, done come and went.
Here it is December and I ain't holdin' a (fence).

It's way after Monday, Tuesday, Wednesday, Thursday, Friday,
    Saturday, Sunday.
Way after one, my daddy ain't come home yet.

"Joogie Blues"

I'm evil, don't know what to do.
I'm evil, 'cause I show it too.
I joogie, joogie, joogie all the time.

Don't play me, don't do no good.
I'm acting, like a block of wood.
All day long it's running through my mind.
I've got the joogie blues, always on my mind.
The joogie blues, I have 'em all the time.
When it's late at night and early morn I always feel 'em comin' on.
I think (I'll hit the dirt), ain't nobody comin' 'round.
But you can't trust nobody at all.
When I cook my frog legs good and brown,
I'll catch my snake and I'll fry him down.
'Cause I've got the joogie, joogie, joogie, I've got those joogie blues.

I've got the joogie blues, always on my mind.
I've got the joogie blues, have 'em all the time.
When it's late at night and early morn, I always feel 'em comin on.
I say I've been filled up, ain't nobody 'round,
That you can trust, nobody at all.
When I cook my frog legs good and brown,
I'll catch my snake and I'll fry him down.
'Cause I've got the joogie, joogie, joogie, 'cause I've got those joogie
    blues.
I say, I've got those joogie blues.
I mean, I've got those joogie blues.

"Ever After On"

Late last night when my baby came home,
I heard a mighty knockin' on my door.
I was up in my stockin' feet, skippin' across the floor.
Tellin' baby, don't you knock no more.

Bring me a pillow for my poor head.
A hammer for to knock out my brains.
The whiskey has ruined this body of mine.
And the red lights has run me insane.
And then what's worse, my mother said,
"My daughter, don't you go astray."
If I had listened to what she said,
I would not be here today.

Oh, ain't it hard, oh, ain't it hard, oh, ain't it hard for a gal to love a
    man don't love you.
Oh, ain't it hard, oh, ain't it hard, oh, ain't it hard for a gal to love a
    man don't love you.

But I love my baby till the sea runs dry.
Till the (rump of doggies tanned by the sun.)
I love my baby till the day he dies
And ever after more.
Oh, ain't it hard, oh, ain't it hard, oh, ain't it hard for a gal to love a
    man don't love you.
Oh, ain't it hard, oh, ain't it hard, oh, ain't it hard for a gal to love a
    man don't love you.

—————— Ma Yancey ——————

Estella, Mama or Ma Yancey was born on January 1, 1896, in Cairo, Illinois (Harris), and died in May, 1986 (liner notes to Atlantic Blues). Ma Yancey married Jimmy Yancey, a talented blues singer and pianist, in 1919, and they remained married until his death in 1951 (Harris). She often performed gigs with her husband, and she worked with many other well known blues men, including Little Brother Montgomery.

Ma Yancey is perhaps most famous for her cover of "How Long Blues," a song on which she is accompanied by her husband on piano. In this song, Ma Yancey feels the blues pulsating within her as her wailing and moaning voice accentuates the heartaches and ailments that lie behind every blues song.

"How Long Blues"

I woke up this mornin' with the blues all around my bed.
Hadn't a been a good woman, the blues would've had me dead.

I have been to the Delta, to the Delta, baby, now, I've done tried.
I can't stand no more trouble than any gal my size.

How long, how long, babe, how long will it be
Before you learn to quit mistreatin' me?

I take you on my rider, baby, to try to teach you right from wrong.
And the more that I talk, baby, the more that you done wrong.

You will not listen to me, babe, you will not listen to my plea.
I am leaving you now and I hope I'll set your heart free.

When I spank you, baby, try to teach you right from wrong.
You will not listen to me, when I look you will be gone.

Now how long, how long, babe, how long will it be
Before you learn to quit mistreatin' me?

I have taken you, baby, I've taken you and I've put you on my right
      side.
And I try to tell you now, baby, time to let me ride.

You will not, you will not do nothin' that I try to tell you to.
So I am switchin' partners and I'm gettin' away from you.

I walk and talk, baby, by myself.
I love you but I just can't help myself.

"Make Me a Pallet on the Floor"

Make me a pallet on your floor.
Make me a pallet on your floor.
Make me a pallet on your floor, a pallet, baby, on your floor.
When your good gal comes home she will never know.

Make it soft and easy, then come get your dough.
Make it soft and easy, then come get your dough.
But when your sweet woman comes, baby, she will never know that
      you made me a pallet on your floor.

I will get up in the mornin' and cook you a red hot meal
I will get up in the mornin' and cook you a red hot meal.
(Just to take what you got me), what you done to me so long when
      you made me a pallet on your floor.

Now I'm gonna sleep there, sleep there far too long.
Now I'm gonna sleep there, I'm gonna sleep there far too long.
If you feel like lying down I don't think she will ever know as long
      as you lay a pallet on the floor.

Just make it good and make it till you fix that dough.
Just make it good and make it till you fix that dough.
The way she comes home, baby, she will never know that you made
      me a pallet on your floor.

Discography

Bogan, Lucille—"Black Angel Blues"; *Rare and Hot 1923–1930*; Historical Records 5829-15 (1929).

"Coffee Grindin' Blues"; *Rare and Hot 1923–1930*; Historical Records 5829-15 (1929).

"Groceries on the Shelf"; *News and the Blues — Telling It Like It Is*; Columbia Records 74-64-46217-1 (1933).

"New Way Blues"; *Blue Ladies 1926–1930*; Southern Preservation Records NR C656 (1928).

"Pay Roll Blues"; *Blue Ladies 1926–1930*; Southern Preservation Records NR C656 (1928).

"Pothound Blues"; *Weed, A Rare Batch*; Stash Records ST-107 (1928).

"Shave 'Em Dry"; *Street Walkin' Blues*; Stash Records ST-117 (1935).

"Stew Meat Blues"; *Straight and Gay*; Stash Records ST-118.

"Tired as I Can Be"; *Them Dirty Blues*; Jass Records (1934).

Brown, Lisa & Johnson, Ann—"Get On Out of Here"; *The Story of the Blues: A Documentary History of the Blues*; Paul Oliver and the E.F. Day Group 66232 CBS (1929).

Carter, Margaret—"Come Get Me Papa Before I Faint"; *Rare and Hot 1923–1930*; Historical Records 5829-15 (1926).

"I Want Plenty of Grease in My Fryin' Pan"; *Rare and Hot 1923–1930*; Historical Records 5829-15 (1926).

Cox, Ida—"Blues Ain't Nothin' But"; *Blues Ain't Nothin' Else But*; Milestone MLP-2015 (1924).

"Blues Ain't Nothin' Else But"; *Blues Ain't Nothin' Else But*; Milestone MLP-2015 (1924).

"Booze Crazy Man"; *Blues Ain't Nothin' Else But*; Milestone MLP-2015 (1928).

"Broadcasting"; *Blues Ain't Nothin' Else But*; Milestone MLP-2015 (1928).

"Chattanooga Blues"; *Blues Ain't Nothin' Else But*; Milestone MLP-2015 (1923).

"Chicago Monkey Man"; *Blues Ain't Nothin' Else But*; Milestone MLP-2015 (1924).

"Cold and Blue"; *Blues Ain't Nothin' Else But*; Milestone MLP-2015 (1927).

"Fogyism"; *Blues Ain't Nothin' Else But*; Milestone MLP-2015 (1928).

"Four Day Creep"; *Stars of the Apollo Theatre*; Columbia KG 30788 (1939).

"How Can I Miss You When I've Got Dead Aim?"; *Blues Ain't Nothin' Else But*; Milestone MLP-2015 (1925).

"How Long, Daddy, How Long"; *Blues Ain't Nothin' Else But*; Milestone MLP-2015 (1925).

"One Time Woman Blues"; *Blues Ain't Nothin' Else But*; Milestone MLP-2015 (1925).

"Pleading Blues"; *Blues Ain't Nothin' Else But*; Milestone MLP-2015 (1927).

"Seven Day"; *Blues Ain't Nothin' Else But*; Milestone MLP-2015 (1927).

Dixon, Mary—"Daddy, You've Got Everything"; *Them Dirty Blues*; Jass Records (1929).

Douglas, Lizzie (Memphis Minnie)—"Caught Me Wrong Again"; *Keep On Goin' 1931–1941*; Document DL P559 (1936).

"Don't Bother It"; *Keep On Goin' 1931–1941*; Document DL P559 (1931).

"Frankie Jean"

"Hustlin' Woman Blues"

"I'm a Bad Luck Woman"; *Keep On Goin' 1931–1941*; Document DL P559 (1936).

"I'm a Gamblin' Woman"; *Keep On Goin' 1931–1941*; Document DL P559 (1936).

"I'm Going Don't You Know"; *Keep On Goin' 1931–1941*; Document DL P559 (1937).

"I'm Waitin' on You"; *Keep On Goin' 1931–1941*; Document DL P559 (1935).

"If You See My Rooster"; *Them Dirty Blues*; Jass Records 1987 (1936).

"Jockey Man Blues"; *Keep On Goin' 1931–1941*; Document DL P559 (1935).

"Keep On Goin'"; *Keep On Goin' 1931–1941*; Document DL P559 (1935).

"Living the Best I Can"; *Keep On Goin' 1931–1941*; Document DL P559 (1937).

"Ma Rainey"; *News and the Blues Telling It Like It Is*; Columbia 74 64-46217.

"No Need You Doggin' Me"; *Keep On Goin' 1931–1941*; Document DL P559 (1937).

"Preacher's Blues"

"Socket Blues"; *Keep On Goin' 1931–1941*; Document DL P559 (1932).

"Today, Today Blues"; *Keep On Goin' 1931–1941*; Document DL P559 (1931).

"When You're Asleep"; *Keep On Goin' 1931–1941*; Document DL P559 (1935).

Fitzgerald, Ella—"When I Get Low I Get High"; *Weed, a Rare Batch;* Stash Records ST 107.

Gibson, Cleo—"I've Got Movements in My Hips"; *The Story of the Blues: A Documentary History of the Blues;* Paul Oliver and the E.F. Day Group 66232 CBS (1929).

Goodner, Lilian—"Four Flushin' Papa"; *Rare and Hot 1923–1926;* Historical Records 5829-14 (1923-6).

"Gonna Get Somebody's Daddy"; *Rare and Hot 1923–1926;* Historical Records 5829-14 (1923-6).

Henderson, Rosa—"Get It Fixed"; *Rare and Hot 1923–1930;* Historical Records 5829-15 (1923-6).

"Somebody's Doin' What You Wouldn't Do"; *Rare and Hot 1923–1926;* Historical Records 5829-14 (1923-6).

Hill, Bertha (Chippie)—"Street Walkin' Blues"; *Street Walkin' Blues;* Stash Records ST 117.

Hunter, Alberta—"Boogie Woogie Swing"; *Alberta Hunter: The Thirties;* Stash Records ST 115 (1940).

"Fine and Mellow"; *Alberta Hunter: The Thirties;* Stash Records ST 115 (1939).

"He's Got a Punch Like Joe Louis"; *Alberta Hunter: The Thirties;* Stash Records ST 115.

"I Won't Let You Down"; *Alberta Hunter: The Thirties;* Stash Records ST 115 (1940).

"I'll See You Go"; *Alberta Hunter: The Thirties;* Stash Records ST 115 (1939).

"Second Hand Man"; *Alberta Hunter: The Thirties;* Stash Records ST 115 (1935).

"Send Me a Man"; *Alberta Hunter: The Thirties;* Stash Records ST 115 (1935).

"Take Your Big Hands Off"; *Alberta Hunter: The Thirties;* Stash Records ST 115.

"The Castle's Rockin'"; *Alberta Hunter: The Thirties;* Stash Records ST 115 (1940).

"Yelpin' the Blues"; *Alberta Hunter: The Thirties;* Stash Records ST 115 (1939).

"You Can't Tell the Difference After Dark"; *Alberta Hunter: The Thirties;* Stash Records St 115 (1935).

Johnson, Lil—"Honey, You're So Good to Me"; *Them Dirty Blues*; Jass Records 1987 (1936).

"Keep Your Hands Off It"; *Straight and Gay*; Stash Records ST 118 (1937).

"My Baby (Squeeze Me Again)"; *Them Dirty Blues*; Jass Records 1987 (1937).

"New Shave 'Em Dry"; *Street Walkin' Blues*; Stash Records ST 117 (1936).

"Press My Button (Ring My Bell)"; *Copulating Blues*; Stash Records ST 101 (1936).

"Stavin' Chain"; *Copulating Blues*; Stash Records ST 101 (1937).

"You Stole My Cherry"; *Copulating Blues*; Stash Records ST 101 (1937).

Johnson, Mary—"Muddy Creek Blues"; *Blue Ladies 1926–1930*; Southern Preservation Records NR C656 (1929).

"Room Rent Blues"; *Blue Ladies 1926–1930*; Southern Preservation Records NR C656 (1929).

Johnson, Robert—"Crossroad Blues"; *Robert Johnson: The Complete Recordings*; Columbia 46233.

Liston, Virginia—"I've Got What It Takes"; *Street Walkin' Blues*; Stash Records ST 117 (1924).

Mae, Lil—"Wise Like That"; *OJL's Georgia*; OJL 25 (1930).

Martin, Sara—"Useless Blues"; *OJL's Georgia*; OJL 25 (1927).

Moore, Alice—"Kidman Blues"; *Blue Ladies 1926–1930*; Southern Preservation Records NR C656 (1930).

"Lonesome Dream Blues"; *Blue Ladies 1926–1930*; Southern Preservation Records NR C656 (1930).

Moore, Monette—"Black Sheep Blues"; *Rare and Hot 1923–1926*; Historical Records 5829-14 (1925).

"Bye Bye Blues"; *Rare and Hot 1923–1926*; Historical Records 5829-14 (1924).

"House Rent Blues"; *Rare and Hot 1923–1926*; Historical Records 5829-14 (1924-25).

"Undertaker Blues"; *Rare and Hot 1923–1926*; Historical Records 5829-14 (1925).

"Workhouse Blues"; *Rare and Hot 1923–1926*; Historical Records 5829-14 (1924).

Myers, Hazel—"Lonesome for That Man of Mine"; *Rare and Hot 1923–1926*; Historical Records 5829-14 (1923-6).

"Pipe Dream Blues"; *Pot, Spoon, Pipe and Jug*; Stash Records ST 102 (1924).

"You'll Never Have No Luck by Quittin' Me"; *Rare and Hot 1923–1926*; Historical Records 5829-14 (1929).

North, Hattie—"Honey Dripper Blues"; *Them Dirty Blues*; Jass Records 1987 (1938).

Pope, Jenny—"Bullfrog Blues"; *Rare and Hot 1923–1930*; Historical Records 5829-15 (1930).

"Tennessee Workhouse Blues"; *Rare and Hot 1923–1930*; Historical Records 5829-15 (1936).

Rainey, Ma—"Blame It on the Blues"; *Blame It On the Blues*; Milestone MLP 2008 (1928).

"Dead Drunk Blues"; *Blame It on the Blues*; Milestone MLP 2008 (1927).

"Hustlin' Blues"; *Blue Ladies 1926–1930*; Southern Preservation Records NR C656 (1928).

"Log Camp Blues"; *Blue Ladies 1926–1930*; Southern Preservation Records NR C656 (1928).

"Moonshine Blues"; *Blame It on the Blues*; Milestone MLP 2008 (1927).

"New Bo-Weevil Blues"; *Blame It on the Blues*; Milestone MLP 2008 (1927).

Ringgold, Issie—"Be on Your Merry Way"; *Blue Ladies 1926–1930*; Southern Preservation Records NR C656 (1930).

"He's a Good Meat Cutter"; *Blue Ladies 1926–1930*; Southern Preservation Records NR C656 (1930).

Scruggs, Irene—"Must Get Mine in Front"; *Street Walkin' Blues*; Stash Records ST 117 (1930).

Smith, Bessie—"Do Your Duty"; *Copulating Blues*; Stash Records ST 101 (1933).

"Gulf Coast Blues"; *Bessie Smith: The Complete Recordings Vol. 1*; Columbia 47307 AAD.

Smith, Bessie & Smith, Clara—"Far Away Blues"; *Bessie Smith: The Complete Recordings Vol. 1*; 47308 AAD.

Smith, Clara—"Courthouse Blues"; *Rare Recordings of the '20s Vol. 1*; CBS 64218 (Printed in Holland) (1925).

"Daddy, Don't Put That Thing on Me"; *Jazzum 2*; Columbia 143231-3 (1929).

"Every Woman's Blues"; *Clara Smith Vol. 1*; CBS Records International (1923).

"I Ain't Got Nobody to Grind My Coffee"; *Jazzum 2*; Columbia 143231-3 (1928).

"Kitchen Mechanic Blues"; *Street Walkin' Blues*; Stash Records ST 117 (1925).

"My John Blues"; *Rare Recordings of the '20s*; CBS 64218 (1925).

"Race Track Blues"; *Jazzum 2*; Columbia 143231-3 (1926).

"Tell Me When"; *Jazzum 2*; Columbia 143231-3 (1929).

"Wanna Go Home"; *Jazzum 2*; Columbia 143231-3 (1928).

"Whip It to a Jelly"; *The Story of the Blues: A Documentary History of the Blues*; Paul Oliver and the E.F. Day Group 66232 CBS (1926).

Smith, Elizabeth—"Gwine to Have Bad Luck for Seven Years"; *Thomas Morris and the Blues Singers*; Retrieval FB 306 (1926).

"Police Done Tore My Playhouse Down"; *Thomas Morris and the Blues Singers*; Retrieval FB 306 (1927).

Smith, Mamie—"Fare Thee Honey Blues"; *Crazy Blues*; Official Records 6037 (1920).

"Frankie Blues"; *Crazy Blues*; Official Records 6037 (1921).

"If You Don't Want Me Blues"; *Crazy Blues*; Official Records 6037 (1920).

"Jazzbo Ball"; *Crazy Blues*; Official Records 6037 (1921).

"Lovin' Sam from Alabam'"; *Crazy Blues*; Official Records 6037 (1920).

"Mem'ries of Mammy"; *Crazy Blues*; Official Records 6037 (1920).

"That Thing Called Love"; *Crazy Blues*; Official Records 6037 (1920).

"The Lure of the South"; *Stars of the Apollo Theatre*; Columbia KG 30788 (1929).

"The Road Is Rocky"; *Crazy Blues*; Official Records 6037 (1920).

"U Need Some Loving Blues"; *Crazy Blues*; Official Records 6037 (1921).

"What Have I Done?"; *Crazy Blues*; Official Records 6037 (1921).

"You Can't Keep a Good Man Down"; *Crazy Blues*; Official Records 6037 (1920).

Smith, Trixie—"Freight Train Blues"; *St Louis Blues*; Serie Cicala (made in Italy) BLJ 8001 (1920).

"I Don't Know and I Don't Care Blues"; *St. Louis Blues*; Serie Cicala (made in Italy) BLJ 8001 (1924).

"Sorrowful Blues"; *St. Louis Blues*; Serie Cicala (made in Italy) BLJ 8001 (1924).

Spivey, Victoria—"Arkansas Road Blues"; *Recorded Legacy of the Blues*; Original Recordings of Spivey Productions LP 2001 (1927).

"Black Snake Blues"; *Straight and Gay*; Stash Records ST 118.

"Christmas Morning Blues"; *The Story of the Blues: A Documentary History of the Blues*; Paul Oliver and the E.F. Day Group 66232 CBS.

"Detroit Moan"; *Recorded Legacy of the Blues*; Original Recordings of Spivey Productions LP 2001 (1936).

"Don't Trust Nobody Blues"; *Recorded Legacy of the Blues*; Original Recordings of Spivey Productions LP 2001 (1931).

"Give It to Him"; *Recorded Legacy of the Blues*; Original Recordings of Spivey Productions LP 2001 (1937).

"How Do You Do It That Way?"; *Recorded Legacy of the Blues*; Original Recordings of Spivey Productions LP 2001 (1929).

"I Can't Last Long"; *Recorded Legacy of the Blues*; Original Recordings of Spivey Productions LP 2001 (1936).

"I'll Keep Sittin' on It (If I Can't Sell It)"; *Copulating Blues*; Stash Records ST 101 (1936).

"Murder in the First Degree"; *Recorded Legacy of the Blues*; Original Recordings of Spivey Productions LP 2001 (1927).

"T.B.'s Got Me"; *Recorded Legacy of the Blues*; Original Recordings of Spivey Productions LP 2001 (1936).

"The Alligator Pond Went Dry"; *Recorded Legacy of the Blues*; Original Recordings of Spivey Productions LP 2001 (1927).

Stewart, Priscilla—"A Little Bit Closer"; *Blue Ladies 1926–1930*; Southern Preservation Records NR C656.

"I Want to See My Baby"; *Blue Ladies 1926–1930*; 1928.

Thomas, Hociel—"Deep Water Blues" *Rare Recordings of the '20s Vol. 4*; CBS 65421 (1926).

"Lonesome Hours"; *Rare Recordings of the '20s Vol. 4*; CBS 65421 (1926).

Wallace, Sippie—"A Jealous Woman Like Me"; *Rare Recordings of the '20s Vol. 4*; CBS 65421 (1926).

"A Man for Every Day of the Week"; *Rare Recordings of the '20s Vol. 4*; CBS 65421 (1926).

"Dead Drunk Blues"; *Rare Recordings of the '20s Vol. 4*; CBS 65421 (1927).

"I Feel Good"; *Rare Recordings of the '20s Vol. 4*; CBS 65421 (1926).

"Jack of Diamond Blues"; *Rare Recordings of the '20s Vol. 1*; CBS 64218 (Printed in Holland).

"The Mail Train Blues"; *Rare Recordings of the '20s Vol. 4*; CBS 65421 (1926).

Walton, Lorraine—"If You're a Viper"; *Weed, A Rare Batch*; Stash Records ST 107.

White, Georgia—"Walkin' the Street"; *Street Walkin' Blues*; Stash Records ST 117 (1937).

Whitmire, Margaret—"T'ain't a Cow in Texas"; *Blue Ladies 1926–1930*; Southern Preservation Records NR C656 (1927).

"That Thing's Done Been Put on Me"; *Blue Ladies 1926–1930*; Southern Preservation Records NR C656 (1927).

Wilson, Edith—"My Handyman Ain't Handy No More"; *Them Dirty Blues*; Jass-Records 1987 (1930).

Winston, Edna—"Ever After On"; *Thomas Morris and the Blues Singers*; Retrieval FB 306.

"I Got a Mule to Ride"; *Thomas Morris and the Blues Singers*; Retrieval FB 306.

"Joogie Blues"; *Thomas Morris and the Blues Singers*; Retrieval FB 306.

"Mama's Gonna Drop Your Curtain"; *Thomas Morris and the Blues Singers*; Retrieval FB 306.

"Pail in My Hand"; *Thomas Morris and the Blues Singers*; Retrieval FB 306.

"Peepin' Jim"; *Thomas Morris and the Blues Singers*; Retrieval FB 306.

"Way After One and My Daddy Ain't Come Home Yet"; *Thomas Morris and the Blues Singers*; Retrieval FB 306.

Yancey, Ma—"How Long Blues"

"Make Me a Pallet on Your Floor"

Works Cited

Carr, Ian, Digby Fairweather, and Brian Priestly. *Jazz the Essential Companion.* New York: Prentice Hall Press, 1987.

Claghorn, Charles E. *Biographical Dictionary of Jazz.* Englewood Cliffs, N.J.: Prentice Hall, 1982.

Dixon, Robert M.W., and John Godrich. *Blues and Gospel Records: 1902-1943.* Essex: Storyville Publications, 1982.

Ellison, Ralph. *Invisible Man.* New York: Vintage Books, 1952.

_____. *Shadow & Act.* New York: New American Library, 1972.

Feather, Leonard. *Encyclopedia of Jazz.* London: Quartet Books, 1960.

Grattan, Virginia L. *American Women Songwriters: A Biographical Dictionary.* Westport, Conn.: Greenwood Press, 1993.

Harris, Sheldon. *The Blues Who's Who: A Biographical Dictionary of Blues Singers.* New Rochelle, N.Y.: Arlington House, 1979.

Harrison, Daphne. *Black Pearls.* New Brunswick, N.J.: Rutgers University Press, 1988.

Herzhaft, Gerard. *Encyclopedia of the Blues.* Fayetteville: University of Arkansas Press, 1992.

Hughes, Langston. "Early Evening Quarrel," in *Selected Poems Langston Hughes.* New York: Vintage Books, 1959.

Hurston, Zora Neale. "Sweat" in *Fire!!: Devoted to Younger Negro Artists.* New York: The Fire!! Press, 1982.

Knight, Etheridge. "My Life the Quality of Which," in *The Essential Etheridge Knight.* Pittsburgh: University of Pittsburgh Press, 1986.

Lomax, Alan. *The Land Where the Blues Began.* New York: Pantheon Books, 1993.

Southern, Eileen. *Biographical Dictionary of Afro-American & African Musicians.* Westport, Conn.: Greenwood Press, 1982.

Thurman, Wallace. *The Blacker the Berry.* New York: Macmillan Publishing Co., 1970.

Wilson, August. *Ma Rainey's Black Bottom: A Play in Two Acts.* New York: New American Library, 1985.

Index of Themes

Index to First Lines

173